DID YOU KNOW

VOL. 1

(For All Bollywood Obsessed Movie Buffs)

51 Interesting Facts about Hindi Cinema

Bobby Sing

notionpress.com

INDIA • SINGAPORE • MALAYSIA

First Published by Notion Press 2014
New Revised & Enhanced Edition Published by Notion Press 2018
Third Edition Published by Notion Press 2024

ISBN 978-93-84391-07-2

….. Dedicated …..

To the Supreme Guiding power

To that young innocent soul who left us all so early,
becoming our loving Angel forever

To my adorable four-legged friend,
watching us from his heavenly abode

&

To all my masters on the path,
who taught me the way to move ahead
in the right spirit with

HIS BLESSINGS

….. *Devoted* …..

To my family,
who might not read what I write,
but knows whatever it is,
has to be something worth doing

&

To my late uncle,
who was the only relative owning
a VCR in that golden era
and allowed me to see as many films as I could,
giving a standing instruction of 'no limit'
to the local video library owner.

This is for you!

A WORD

..... WITH MY FELLOW CINEMA LOVERS .....

As the title of the book was being decided, someone suggested the word *'Trivia'* which is more often used for describing such interesting information or write-ups. I looked upon the word's actual meaning in the dictionary and it said: *unimportant facts or details.* Discovering that, my first reaction was 'No, this is not the word to describe the 51 chapters included in this book,' as this is nothing unimportant, ignorable, or gossip, but rather quite relevant and fascinating revelation of facts that every die-hard Hindi cinema follower would love to know and think upon.

Moreover, this is a book both for friends who just enjoy movies as an essential part of their weekend entertainment and then for the 'my types,' who eat, drink, sleep and think cinema all the time like a mad, passionate lover of this specific art form.

No doubt, the new-age gadgets like laptops, tablets, and mobile phones have toned down the way cinema used to be cherished a few decades back just on the big screen. Yet the madness has not died and the passion is still alive in a different form today, stored in the small hard disks through the powerful digital media opening many new avenues.

Yes, the quality of our Hindi films has suffered and the over-commercialisation of the stream has arguably turned them all into mere well-marketed, short-lived products in this present Internet age. Still, hope is alive and many young enthusiastic minds are also willing to bring back that enigmatic magic on the silver screen through their individual efforts.

As a humble contribution in the same direction, this is to highlight many astonishing facts about Hindi cinema that might help as well as inspire the new aspiring filmmakers ready for that next major breakthrough, to look into our cherished 'golden past' with much more love and reverence.

Also, many thanks to the Notion Press team for their complete support and for being patient with the never-ending changes in the cover layout and text. Grateful to all my Facebook/Twitter/Instagram friends for their constant encouragement and to Jaspreet Singh Sahni for his valuable time spent reading/editing the text repeatedly.

Though I have taken extreme care in quoting the names and dates included in the 51 chapters, would truly appreciate your valuable feedback, in case you find any conflicts in the facts shared.

I hope the attempt reaches its target audience and meets the expectations of all fellow cinema lovers and well-wishers.

Cheers to the passion forever,

Bobby Sing *(Harpreet)*

bobbytalkscinema.com

(*Note:* For friends, wondering where the 'h' has gone from my last name 'Singh' as it is usually written. It has nothing to do with numerology as many might be thinking. Rather, it is an innovation tried in the early part of my career beginning from musical stage shows (as a singer) and the passion is here to stay till the end cherishing the gift of existence. So the 'Sing' in the name actually denotes 'Singing' or 'Gaana'.......... with *His Blessings.*)

About DID YOU KNOW Series

Documentation and archiving had never been our priority in the last century and cinema was never considered as the nation's cultural heritage to be duly written about and preserved for the future generations. This remains the major reason why we did not record or document the first-hand experiences of our great filmmakers and the making of their cult films. Not much was researched or written in the form of books when the maestros were still with us and thus the write-ups in reputed film magazines remained the only source of reliable information apart from a few relevant books on the subject.

Thankfully, the new millennium witnessed a major boost in the publication of books based on Hindi cinema, and at present, we have many worth reading and recommended works exploring the Golden Era, the maestros, and their ageless creations, along with the new-age gems and the filmmakers of the present times.

Having said that, I personally found these books targeting only the knowledgeable readers, the connoisseurs, who are already familiar with their cinema, the music, and its deeper aspects. I honestly did not find any book specifically written for movie lovers from the younger generation, who are not really acquainted with our golden past. A book written in simple language introducing the readers to our rich cinematic heritage with some interesting facts and anecdotes inspiring them to experience the sheer magic was sadly missing.

So DID YOU KNOW series is specifically conceived for all the young friends, who are more than eager to know about the present as well as the past classics of our Hindi cinema, and the lesser-known stories related to their making.

However, the series is not about any filmy gossip, relationships between the stars, or unconfirmed backstage stories leading to controversies. It majorly focuses on films and the facts you can witness on screen by simply watching them on YouTube or an online movie portal.

Hope the book reaches the maximum young readers and it proves a worth-exploring, useful series for all the true movie-buffs.

Bobby Sing *(Harpreet)*

bobbytalkscinema.com

CONTENTS

(The 51 chapters of this book have been divided into three sections. While the first features facts about Hindi films before the '90s, i.e., before the cable TV revolution entered India, the second talks about the link between the two eras and the third is about the movies post the '90s.)

SECTION ONE

SECTION TWO

SECTION THREE

Section One

CHAPTER ONE

Satyajit Ray – A Rare Phenomenon

A name that needs no introduction for anyone even remotely familiar with Indian cinema, Satyajit Ray made only two Urdu/Hindi films along with all the world-famous Bengali classics in his illustrious career. But no cinematic discussion can ignore his gigantic contribution to the medium and there is a specific purpose why the first chapter of the book has been dedicated to him, clearing a major misconception about his films and the thought behind the director's selection of genres.

Meeting many established as well as young entrants in the field, I realized that most of them had a huge misconception that Satyajit Ray made films only on poverty and stories revolving around the poor and rural regions depicting their social issues.

That is one of the greatest myths, as the maestro has such a wide range of genres in his celebrated repertoire and never remained confined to any specific one right from the beginning.

So, with a motive of clearing the doubts, I would simply like to list here the exceptional creative abilities and achievements of this gifted personality, which would evidently state why he is being referred to as '*a rare phenomenon*' in the heading. Plus, these enlightening facts will be inviting enough for all young movie buffs to get hooked on the world of meaningful, thought-provoking, and unforgettable films made by the visionary director.

1. Satyajit Ray made his first movie *Pather Panchali* (Bengali) in 1955 on a very limited budget (with invaluable financial help also coming from Kishore Kumar) and the film now finds its place in the list of '*100 Best Movies In The World of Cinema*' all over the globe without any exception.
2. Before becoming a filmmaker, he worked in an advertising agency as a creative visualiser/graphic designer for more than a decade and later used the same experience in creating delightful artwork, posters, and booklets for his films.
3. Possibly the first ever person who worked in almost every department associated with film-making, be it drawing storyboards, script writing, dialogues, costume designing, camerawork, editing, directing, and even composing music, background score, and conducting studio recordings.
4. Other than being a filmmaker, Ray was a prolific writer who has several collections of short stories, including many especially written for kids with famous characters like '*Prof. Shonku*'. His stories are full of supernatural stuff, mysteries, and small pleasures of life and are equally enjoyable for everyone irrespective of any region, language, or age.

5. He also revived *'Sandesh'*, a children's magazine founded by his grandfather, to which he contributed illustrations, write-ups, and stories till the last phase of his life.
6. Apart from making socially relevant films, satirical comedies, documentaries, and insightful cinema (in Bengali), Ray is the creator of a hugely famous detective series too, featuring *'Feluda'* as the intelligent investigator. The character is not only popular among young readers but has many grown-ups also addicted to its engaging stories. It also finds its place among the bestselling detective series in the publishing world in India. In fact, Ray himself directed two feature films based on *Feluda's* adventures, namely *Sonar Kella* (1974) and *Joi Baba Felunath* (1979). Later, other filmmakers, including his son Sandip Ray, also adapted his *Feluda* adventures for many more films.
7. In his detective series, Ray also made a film *Chiriyakhana* (1967) on another of Bengal's immensely famous fictional detectives *Byomkesh Bakshi,* featuring Uttam Kumar in the lead role.
8. Ray made only two Urdu/Hindi films in his career, which were *Shatranj Ke Khiladi* in 1977 (including extensive use of Urdu and English) and a short film *Sadgati* in 1981 for Doordarshan. Both these films were based on the stories of Munshi Premchand.
9. Two of his unmade projects include one revolving around 'an alien' and the other a musical documentary on the world-renowned sitarist Pandit Ravi Shankar, which has also been released in the form of a book, including its complete visual storyboard with sketches by Ray in water colours. Amazingly, one of his short stories 'Bonkubabu's Friend' and his works on the project 'The Alien' is said to be quite close and perhaps the basic thought behind

Steven Spielberg's *E.T. The Extra-Terrestrial* released in 1982.

10. Satyajit Ray is the only Indian who has been awarded *The Lifetime Achievement OSCAR* in recognition of his rare mastery in the art of motion pictures. Unfortunately, Ray had suffered a heart attack and was confined to bed when the award was announced at the beginning of 1992. He received the honour at his hospital bed in Calcutta (now Kolkata), through a special satellite-television event arranged by the Academy.
11. Interestingly, apart from many other reputed awards, Indian Government also honoured Satyajit Ray with the *Bharat Ratna*, the highest civilian award in India, post the Academy recognition.

The great soul died on April 23, 1992, after a long illness but he continues to live through his movies to date and will remain in our memories forever as a true master of his art.

So, in case you also believed that Satyajit Ray only made movies on poverty and stories about rural India, then get rid of the misconception and witness the magic of his films beginning from *Shatranj Ke Khiladi*, which is probably the only Hindi film revolving around the game of chess and its two passionate players.

❖ ❖ ❖

Fact File: The myth about Satyajit Ray films exploiting poverty in India originated from Nargis Dutt's statement given in the Rajya Sabha assembly in the year 1980, which was later strongly condemned by the film fraternity. Nargis was the first actress from the Hindi film industry to be nominated as a Rajya Sabha Member.

CHAPTER TWO

Bimal Roy, Gulzar and William Shakespeare

Every true lover of Hindi cinema must have seen the classic comedy *Angoor* several times, enjoying its well-directed and superbly-enacted comic sequences featuring Sanjeev Kumar, Deven Verma, Moushmi Chatterjee and Deepti Naval in the lead roles. The 1982 film, written & directed by Gulzar, was a fine adaptation of William Shakespeare's play *'The Comedy of Errors'* and is now unanimously included in every must-watch list of critics as well as viewers for Hindi comedy movies.

However, the interesting fact is that the same story plot based on Shakespeare's play was earlier used by Gulzar's mentor Bimal Roy in his 1968 produced film *Do Dooni Chaar* directed by Debu Sen. The black and white film featuring Kishore Kumar & Asit Sen in double roles (of twin brothers), similar to Sanjeev Kumar and Deven Verma in *Angoor* had many enjoyable sequences depicting the comic theme. Though the conclusion is subjective, Gulzar's version of the famous play was indeed a much more entertaining venture compared to Debu Sen's vintage classic that also had the famous melodious song *"Hawaon Pe Likh Do, Hawaon Ke Naam"* composed by Hemant Kumar and sung by Kishore Kumar.

Still, *Do Dooni Chaar* deserves to be seen by every keen student of cinema to witness two different yet positive approaches towards the same subject. Also, as it had both lyrics and dialogues by Gulzar, being an important member of veteran Bimal Roy's creative team working as his assistant. In fact, he was also the chief assistant director to Debu Sen in *Do Dooni Chaar* and it is indeed a remarkable feature of his sparkling career that Gulzar conceived one of the all-time best comedies of Hindi cinema despite being known for more thoughtful, social, and artistic movies.

Another triumph of *Angoor* is its brilliant, light-hearted tribute paid to Shakespeare in the film's introduction and end – a rare feature not usually seen in such adaptations.

Continuing his association with William Shakespeare, Gulzar later also contributed to writer-composer-director Vishal Bhardwaj's trilogy on Shakespeare's famous creations in *Maqbool-Macbeth* (2003), *Omkara-Othello* (2006) and *Haider-Hamlet* (2014) as a lyricist.

❖ ❖ ❖

Fact File: Incidentally, *Do Dooni Chaar* is also supposed to be inspired by the 1963 Bengali film *Bhranti Bilas* (meaning Illusion of Illusion) based on a play by Ishwar Chandra Vidyasagar, which was itself inspired by Shakespeare's *The Comedy of Errors*. The film was directed by Manu Sen and featured Uttam Kumar, Bhanu Bandopadhyay, Sabitri Chatterjee, and Sandhya Roy in the lead (with Uttam Kumar also being the producer).

CHAPTER THREE

The Ageless GUIDE and its English version

Universally quoted as one of the prestigious Hindi films representing Indian cinema all over the world, *Guide* (1966) is a stalwart in the 100-year history of our cinema and is widely considered a textbook material on various aspects of film-making. Its outstanding soundtrack is included among the best musical scores composed for a film to date and the cult movie has a huge global fan-following even today.

However, very few among the younger generation are aware of the fact that *Guide* was first actually made as a 120-minute English film for Western audiences in collaboration with writer Pearl S. Buck (of *The Good Earth* (1937) fame) and director Tad Danielewski. It was not a dubbed film as many might be thinking but was shot as a complete English movie with all the dialogues impressively delivered in English by the entire Indian cast.

It seems to be a clear masterstroke of destiny as Dev Anand began both the English and Hindi versions together to be shot simultaneously, directed by two different directors – Tad Danielewski and Chetan Anand (with Raj Khosla also being an early consideration). But things didn't work out well as both had different visions of the script and wished to shoot it in their own individual way. So, a quick decision was taken to finish the English version first and then work on the Hindi one later as per Chetan Anand's vision with a rewritten script.

Waheeda Rehman became the chosen female lead post the consideration/recommendation of Vyjayanthimala (for being a trained dancer) and Priya Rajvansh (for being well-versed in English). Training sessions, for both language and dance, were arranged for her and the actress came up with one of the finest performances of Hindi cinema to date, as quoted by prominent authors, columnists, and historians.

Unfortunately, the English version didn't work in the international market despite being a big collaboration with many renowned names. Probably that was the reason why it got a very limited release in India at some key centres witnessing an expectedly poor response. Surprisingly, there happened to be one silver lining among the dark clouds as the film won Waheeda Rehman the Best Actress award at the Chicago Film Festival, the news of which came too late to even Waheeda, as revealed by the actress in the book *'Conversation with Waheeda Rehman'* by Nasreen Munni Kabir.

Taking some important lessons from *Guide's* failure in the international market, many substantial changes were made in its storyline suiting the Indian temperament and traditions (with due permission from the author), and then the much-appreciated Hindi version was directed by Vijay Anand in place of his elder brother Chetan, who was then involved in the epic war film *Haqeeqat*.

The new script of *Guide* (Hindi) followed a completely different outlook presenting the same storyline and probably this was one of those rare instances where a similar plot was shot by two different directors with their own perspectives in two entirely different films with the same star cast based on the same novel. The basic theme of the story dealing with adultery was also toned down a lot in the new screenplay because Dev and Waheeda were even shown in bed in the absence of her husband, Kishore Sahu, in the English version.

Still, the film faced a few strange objections from the government authorities who considered it to be quite bold for Indian society, ignoring the fact that the same novel had earlier been given the *Sahitya Akademi Award* by the Indian government itself for the Best Works in English Language in the year 1960. The film finally got released after the intervention of Indira Gandhi, the then Information and Broadcast Minister.

According to a few reports, R.K. Narayan, the original writer of the famous award-winning novel *The Guide* (on which the film was based), was not satisfied with any of the attempts made in the two different languages. But Dev denied any such response from the author in an interview and revealed that he actually liked the English version but then somehow changed his statement post its failure at the box office. Later, Narayan also accepted the Filmfare award for Best Story bagged by the Hindi version, which had many significant changes made by Vijay Anand.

The Indian audience simply loved the Hindi version with all the thoughtful changes made, including an evergreen soundtrack, and the film majorly worked at the box office having a different ending. It was also the first colour film of Dev's career, in which he wasn't playing the character of a typical hero. In fact, the making of the film certainly deserves a detailed book, sharing the chain of events revealed by Dev, Waheeda, and *Guide's* other team members in their respective interviews.

Sadly, the English version was never made available in the home video market, but thankfully it can now be seen on YouTube, uploaded by an enthusiastic Dev Anand fan. The film gives you a great nostalgic experience watching Dev Anand, Waheeda Rehman, Kishore Sahu, Leela Chitnis, and others delivering their dialogues in English, putting up a rare, path-breaking and one-of-its-kind shows in the history of Hindi Cinema.

At the same time, *The Guide* (English) also wasn't any great film in terms of execution and presentation of an extremely complex theme dealing with adultery, glamour, fame, poverty, drought, and spirituality altogether. Moreover, the film also had many sequences specifically inserted to impress the foreign audience, introducing India to them as a country of mystics, snake charmers, and impoverished life in villages. No doubt it couldn't impress anyone abroad or back home when it was released at only a few selected centres.

❖ ❖ ❖

Fact File: *The Guide* in English did not have any songs but a fabulous background score grabbing the attention of its viewers from the very first scene itself. The music was *composed by* S. D. Burman and *conducted by* Rahul and Manohari (as duly mentioned in its credits).

Making a largely unknown revelation in the book mentioned above, Waheeda informs us that before Dev Anand, it was Satyajit Ray who wished to make a film on R. K. Narayan's novel *Guide.* And it was Ray, who first asked her to read the novel a year before Dev came up with the idea. Both Padmini and Leela Naidu were also keen on the role but interestingly, even Ray's first choice for *Rozy* was none other than Waheeda Rehman.

CHAPTER FOUR

Dilip Kumar's strange animal friend in KOHINOOR

Many successful Hindi movies became more famous for the special animal friends of their lead hero and are still remembered for the same even after decades. These adorable friends have always been there with our filmy heroes either to showcase their soft humanitarian side or to play a significant role in the script as a major part of its supporting cast helping the stars in their difficult times.

But yes, in the present new-age cinema, this particular feature of our movies is seldom seen in the more glamourized, VFX-based projects eyeing only the first few days of their release. Still, as we speak of the subject, one can easily recall films such as *Haathi Mere Saathi, Teri Meharbaniyan, Mard, Coolie, Maine Pyar Kiya, Parivaar, Maa, Yateem, Aankhen, Entertainment* and more focusing on these speechless friends. As a matter of fact, Manmohan Desai – the man who was known to catch the pulse of Indian audiences by providing them wholesome entertainment, often had such animal friends featuring alongside his heroes, impressing the target audience.

However, the interesting difference between the above and the one mentioned in the heading remains the uniqueness of the chosen friend who happens to be the only example in the history of Hindi cinema. Putting in specific words, we have seen friends of our heroes ranging from a dog, horse, elephant, pigeon, parrot, monkey, snake, and even an eagle in some highly successful films at the box office. But the black and white classic *Kohinoor* released in 1960 featured the veteran actor Dilip Kumar having a very unusual and strange kind of animal friend - a *mongoose* (known as *nevala* in Hindi), which is the only on-screen appearance of the animal as the hero's companion.

One finds it both novel and strange seeing Dilip Kumar making his entry in the film with his *mongoose* friend sitting on his shoulders tied from the neck with a string. Later in the film, it also saves the master's life by killing a snake released to bite Dilip Kumar.

Undoubtedly, it was a weird but interesting and brave choice made by director S. U. Sunny, never repeated again in any Hindi film.

CHAPTER FIVE

Bertrand Russell and his rare cameo in *Aman*

Bertrand Russell – the eminent mathematician, philosopher, social critic, and political activist – has probably played only one cameo in a film and that was in the courageous, message-oriented, anti-war Hindi movie made in 1967, titled *Aman*.

The film is about a young Indian doctor who, after receiving his medical degree from London, wishes to go to Japan to help the nuclear attack victims of Hiroshima and Nagasaki. He goes there against his father's wish and devotes his life to treating the patients suffering in a very terrible state. After a while, the doctor himself becomes the victim of nuclear reactions and his untimely death turns him into a martyr both in Japan and among his own countrymen back in India.

An insightful project on world peace, *Aman* is a unique and appreciable attempt made without caring about the Box Office returns, which has honestly become a very rare feature of Indian films in the present times. Since the project was being made with noble intentions of sending a global message against the use of nuclear arms, Bertrand Russell agreed to feature in it for a scene as he was himself actively working against the serious issue for years.

Coming to this particular scene, the young doctor played by Rajendra Kumar meets the Nobel Prize winner one to one and listens to his few words of wisdom on world peace. Russell begins talking about the same in English but then a Hindi (voice-over) explanation takes over to make the message understandable for the Indian audience.

Produced and directed by Mohan Kumar, *Aman* featured Rajendra Kumar, Chetan Anand, Balraj Sahni, Saira Banu, Om Prakash, Sajjan, and many foreign artists too in the supporting cast. Shot mostly in locations abroad, it had cinematography by Radhu Karmakar, music by Shankar Jaikishen, and lyrics by Hasrat Jaipuri and Shailendra, along with Prem Dhawan who specifically wrote a soulful poem for a certain Hiroshima Museum sequence in the film.

As the protagonist unfortunately dies in the climax, the film ends with the shot of his body being cremated and Mohd. Rafi sings three lines conveying a message to live with love and harmony to the world. Interestingly, the climax shot of the body being carried by the mourners was also the debut shot of veteran Nasseruddin Shah *(as mentioned in his memoirs).*

As a humble tribute, I have tried to complete the verse by adding a fourth line, hoping that our future is more peaceful than the past and we will not commit the same ugly mistakes ever again in the coming years. The thoughtful verse says:

"Yeh Nafrat Ke Jazbon Mein Hargiz Na Behna,
Meri Baat Sun Lo Galey Mil Ke Rehna,
Jalti Chita Se Yeh Aawaz Aayi,
Meri Maut Pe Sabko Itna Hi Kehna"

CHAPTER SIX

JEEVAN NAIYA AND JHOOLA – THE TWO EARLIER FILMS HAVING THE HIT SONGS, *KOI HAMDAM NA RAHA* AND *EK CHATUR NAAR*

Hindi film music lovers are well familiar with two memorable gems from the golden era – *Koi Humdam Na Raha* and *Ek Chatur Naar* from the films *Jhumroo* (1961) and *Padosan* (1968) respectively. The songs have a huge fan following due to their melodious compositions, impressive lyrics, and fabulous renditions by the masters, led from the front by the legendary Kishore Kumar.

However, not many know that these two songs were originally composed by a Parsi lady music director Saraswati Devi in two successful films released before India's independence and were originally sung by one of the first big stars of Hindi films, Ashok Kumar, in his unique style.

The song *Koi Humdam Na Raha* was earlier there in *Jeevan Naiya* (1936) and the movie was directed by Frank Osten. Ashok Kumar and Devika Rani played the lead roles in the film which had its music composed by Saraswati Devi with lyrics written by J. S. Kashyap and this particular song was sung by Ashok Kumar himself both on and behind the screen.

Later, the same track was used by Dada Muni's (Ashok Kumar) younger brother Kishore Kumar in his film *Jhumroo* (1961) with added lyrics by Majrooh, in which Kishore not only played the lead along with Madhubala but also composed the musical score and gave his voice to the song too in his unmatched style. Directed by Shankar Mukerji, it had a couple of other famous songs penned by Kishore Kumar (including the title track) and the rest by Majrooh Sultanpuri.

As told by Ashok Kumar in an interview, Kishore liked the song from his childhood days and later recorded the same in his film challenging his elder brother that he would sing it better, even if it was a difficult composition and in an odd taal (rhythm/beats). Kishore flawlessly rendered the song that became a big hit and at present, the rendition the whole world is more familiar with is the one sung by Kishore that happens to be a kind of 'version song'.

The second immensely popular track *Ek Chatur Naar* was first heard in Bombay Talkies Ltd presentation *Jhoola* (1941), which was directed by Gyan Mukerji and had Ashok Kumar and Leela Chitnis in the lead. The music of the film was again composed by Saraswati Devi with lyrics by Pradeep and here too Ashok Kumar sang a very short version of the song on the screen as well as on the microphone, giving it a comic touch. The sequence had him hurriedly singing the lines while taking a bath.

After almost three decades, the same track went through a huge transformation in the film *Padosan* (1968), which was directed by Jyoti Swaroop and had Sunil Dutt, Kishore Kumar, Mehmood and Saira Banu playing the lead roles. The music was composed by R. D. Burman with lyrics by Rajindra Krishan and it seems here too Kishore was responsible for the inclusion of this song originally sung by Ashok Kumar. Still, what R. D. Burman eventually did with the basic composition, featuring maestros Kishore Kumar and Manna Dey together as musical rivals (along with Mehmood), took the track to another level and turned it into a cult comic song to be cherished forever.

For records, the team used two other compositions of the past while improvising in the *Padosan* song. One was *"Chanda Re, Ja Re Ja Re"* from the film *Ziddi* (1948) sung by Lata Mangeshkar, composed by Khemchand Prakash and written by Prem Dhawan. In *the Padosan* track, Kishore Kumar sings it as *"Kaala Re, Ja Re Ja Re"* to tease Mehmood. *Ziddi* was also the debut film of Kishore Kumar as a playback singer (again becoming an important contributing link).

The second composition was *'Ban Chale Ram Raghurai'* from *Sant Tulsidas* (1939) directed by Jayant Desai. Sung by Vishnupant Pagnis, the original lyrics were written by Pandit Indra and it was composed by Gyan Dutt. It was adapted as *'Arey Dekhi Teri Chaturai'* by Kishore Kumar in the *Padosan* song.

Besides, the phrase *"Barh Ke Budhan Cheer Bhi Chakkar"* included in the track was inspired by a similar phrase earlier sung by Kishore Kumar in *"Aankh Seedhi Lagi"* - the innovative song in his film *Half Ticket* (1962).

That is the history behind these immensely popular gems of Hindi film music and in case you wish to listen to all the original tracks in their earlier versions, then just log on to YouTube and cherish the classic creations by the masters searching by their respective titles.

CHAPTER SEVEN

Music Director Duos and Laxmikant Pyarelal - From Assistants to Masters

There is an interesting trend of forming a team of two persons as music directors in the Hindi film industry. The origin of this tradition goes back to the black-and-white era (possibly coming from the Qawaali tradition of having two lead singers) and some of the most famous evergreen songs were born to different music director duos, still fondly remembered by true Hindi film music lovers all over the world.

The trend probably began in the early '40s with Husnlal-Bhagatram and later three of the most famous and immensely successful music director duos of the industry were Shankar-Jaikishan, Kalyanji-Anandji and Laxmikant-Pyarelal in their respective eras of the last century. Such was the trend of a music composer duo in that particular era that reportedly a few solo music directors kept deceptive names just to give an impression of two people working together as a team like Shyamji Ghanshyamji and more.

Talking specifically about Laxmikant Pyarelal, very few know the amazing truth that before coming into the limelight, the duo used to work as assistants to Kalyanji-Anandji during the initial phase of their careers (joining them with *Chhalia*) and before that had worked for many other reputed music directors as musicians and arrangers. Their loving relationships with other composers continued even after becoming music directors, and that is the reason R. D. Burman played harmonica in *Dosti* and the duo assisted him in the arrangement for his initial films, including *Chhote Nawab* and *Bhoot Bangla.*

Later, forming a perfect team, Laxmikant was more inclined towards composing (apart from being an excellent mandolin player) and Pyarelal towards the arrangements (along with being an exceptional violinist) as per the requirement. However, they both composed the tunes together to be later selected with mutual consent.

As a matter of fact, Pyarelal is considered to be one of the top five arrangers in the history of Hindi film music with an outstanding knowledge of Indian musical instruments and traditional arrangements. Yet surprisingly, one of the most successful soundtracks of their career remains Subhash Ghai's *Karz* (1980), which had its major tracks solely based on Pop music with complete Western arrangement and sound design (along with a fabulous ghazal, a love song, and a qawwali too).

LP, as the duo was popularly known, were nominated for the Best Music Director for their very first film *Parasmani* itself in 1963, but it was *Dosti* for which they got their first Filmfare award released in 1964. Since then, they were nominated almost every year for their successful musical scores for more than a decade.

The trend of music director duo later continued with Shiv-Hari, Sonik-Omi, Amar-Utpal, Uttam-Jagdish, Nadeem-Shravan,

Anand-Milind, Dilip Sen-Sameer Sen, Jatin-Lalit, (the unique) Ram-Laxman, Sanjeev-Darshan and more. It's still prevalent in the recent era with names such as Salim-Sulaiman, Vishal-Shekhar, Sajid-Wajid, Sachin-Jigar, Ajay-Atul, and even a trio as Shankar-Ehsaan-Loy.

❖ ❖ ❖

Fact File: Hindi film music has witnessed many individuals becoming renowned music directors after working as assistants contributing to several memorable soundtracks. However, Laxmikant-Pyarelal is probably the only musician duo continuing their journey from assistants to masters as a team, thereby setting a rare example.

In the years when both Laxmikant Pyarelal and Kalyanji Anandji were actively working in the industry, a rare instance was seen when, in a film, both were credited together for different musical contributions.

In Subhash Ghai's *Krodhi* (1981), the opening credits mentioned 'Songs Composed and Conducted by Laxmikant Pyarelal' and 'Background Music - Kalyanji Anandji'.

CHAPTER EIGHT

Dilip Kumar's Flawless rendition of a classical composition in MUSAFIR

Words fall short when one writes about one of the greatest actors in the history of Hindi cinema, the legendary Dilip Kumar. The veteran needs no introductory lines or mention of his commendable achievements in a splendid career span of almost half a century.

However, despite having seen his famous epic movies more than once, many die-hard fans of the maestro still might not be informed about the one instance when he unbelievably rendered a classical song in the late '50s. That also means Tapan Sinha's *Sagina* (1974) and Subhash Ghai's *Karma* (1986) are not the only films where Dilip Kumar gave his voice to a song (in the opening lines or interlude). He did sing before, a rather difficult traditional *raag*-based composition, in his film titled *Musafir* in the year 1957.

Interestingly, *Musafir*, which was a light-hearted and simple movie about three different families coming to live in the same rented house one by one, had its important value for a few other reasons as well.

It was Hrishikesh Mukherjee's first film as a director after working with Bimal Roy as an editor. It was also the first Hindi film for the comedian Keshto Mukherjee. Besides, it had a fabulously talented team working together, with Salil Choudhary as the music director, Ritwik Ghatak as the scriptwriter (along with Hrishikesh Mukherjee), dialogues by Rajinder Singh Bedi and lyrics by Shailendra. Written (story), produced, and directed by Hrishikesh Mukherjee, the film also had Suchitra Sen, Durga Khote, Nirupa Roy, Kishore Kumar, Nazir Hussain, David and more playing the key roles.

Returning to our main focus here, it is said that after listening to Dilip Kumar humming something, composer Salil Choudhary asked him to sing along with Lata Mangeshkar for a sequence in the film. Agreeing with the thought (probably because of the respect felt for the master composer), Dilip Kumar performed the song confidently and the rendition came out to be a truly touching one with great depth and feel as if it had been perfectly sung by a trained exponent of classical music.

The song had the words *Laagi Naahin Chhootey Chahey Jiya Jaaye,* and you can thankfully hear the track through numerous uploads on the web (besides watching the entire film). Listening to it for the first time, you probably would not believe that this is the thespian singing himself, but it's indeed a pleasant and surprising truth that needs to be told to highlight another hidden talent of the evergreen legend Dilip Kumar.

CHAPTER NINE

Rajesh Khanna and Phantom in BUNDAL BAAZ - A film directed by Shammi Kapoor

The world of comics is indeed fascinating for kids and teenagers even in the present age of technology and computers. Though the passion may not be as intense as it used to be in the last century in the absence of all currently available alternative mediums of entertainment, still comics do have their share of die-hard fans and enthusiastic lovers who continue to enjoy the colourful pictorial strips and their favourite characters even today.

In fact, there is a big energetic circle of many like-minded friends in almost every city of India (and abroad too) who are still crazy about collecting old editions of comics from the decades of the '70s, '80s, and '90s. Here, although a few of those famous series are still being released in the market in a new format and style, most have become rare and are now being sold at a very high price by a few collectors turned dealers.

Such was the craze of these hugely famous comics in those days that even superstars like Rajesh Khanna supported a small sequence of *Phantom* (*Vaitaal* in Hindi) in his movie called *Bundal Baaz* released in the year 1976. The film was directed by the legendary Shammi Kapoor and was inspired by the world-renowned Arabian tale of *Alladin and His Magical Lamp* from the book *One Thousand and One Nights* (*Arabian Nights*). Even its original soundtrack composed by R. D. Burman had a special instrumental track titled *Phantom Music*. However, while Rajesh Khanna's double played *Phantom* on the screen with a tight body-hugging outfit in blue, the role of *Giant Ginnie* (*Jinn*) was played by Shammi Kapoor himself quite joyfully.

Following the passionate impact of comics in that era, the film straight away begins with this specially inserted sequence featuring the superstar as *Phantom*, catching a few criminals running away after looting a bank. His dog is shown informing him in his skull-like den (along with the film credits) and then *Phantom* rides his famous white horse following the culprits on busy roads of Mumbai (then Bombay) like a true hero. Further, at the end of this sequence, Rajesh Khanna is also shown holding the English edition of *Indrajal Comics* titled, *The Secret Cave of Kings* with *Phantom* riding his horse on its cover.

To be honest, I enjoy watching this rare amalgamation of passion for films and comics on the screen repeatedly and I am sure all the die-hard comics-loving friends will also cherish the same catching the film again.

CHAPTER TEN

YAADEIN – A FIRST OF ITS KIND, UNIQUE, DARING ATTEMPT IN INDIAN CINEMA

Sunil Dutt, a lovable person, is fondly remembered by everyone not only as a film personality but also as a kind, humble, and thoughtful human who had a multi-dimensional career ranging from an actor-producer-director to a social activist-politician. However, it might be news to many that the thinking man was also the first person to make an innovative and first-of-its-kind daring venture in the Hindi film industry, called *Yaadein,* in the year 1964.

The film was a unique attempt since it was a soliloquy act performed by Dutt, in the role of a worried loving husband who is surprised to see his wife and children not at home one day after he returns from work. Making his own assumptions, he starts imagining the reasons for their absence and in turn begins talking to himself mentioning his own mistakes and regrets of the past. The attempt was, and is still, novel because it has only one actor in the movie who talks to himself and his imaginary personalities throughout its nearly two-hour duration on a single set. That is the reason the film remains a path-breaking and experimental piece of art (in black and white), directed by the legendary Sunil Dutt himself as his directorial debut under the banner of Ajanta Arts.

Apart from its solo act, *Yaadein* also remains a must-watch movie for every serious student of cinema for its brilliant emotional sequences and the intelligent use of background music, voice-overs, photographs, cartoons, images, and shadows to show the presence of the other person in its narration. The film also introduces you to another form of visual expression – a silhouette, in which a dark shadow is used to depict a distinct personality on the screen along with the lead character. Based on a story by Mrs. Sunil Dutt (Nargis), the film begins with an important excerpt from *Manu Smriti,* saying:

"The homes where women are respected are visited by Gods to their delight.

But where women are not respected, even the good actions of other members become fruitless."

Reportedly a record-holder in the category of 'fewest actors in a narrative film' and winner of two Filmfare awards (cinematography and sound), *Yaadein* begins with the caption "World's first one actor movie." The film has dialogues by Akhtar-Ul-Iman, lyrics by Anand Bakshi, and music by Vasant Desai, together creating a not-to-be-missed gem if you are really interested in experiencing the 'not so famous' experimental kind of movies made by the courageous Indian film-makers of the yesteryears. But while watching it, do remember that it is not a usual story-telling kind of project made to entertain the viewers and might turn out to be an oddball in the current fast-paced world of electronic gadgets and the Internet. It moves very slowly, becomes monotonous at times with only one man on the screen, and even less interesting after a while.

Yet it can undoubtedly be rated as one of the most innovative and insightful classics of Hindi cinema, made by a creative man who had an infectious smile, a thinking mind, a sensitive soul, and a golden heart – Sunil Dutt.

CHAPTER ELEVEN

Dev Anand was the lead hero of a Hollywood film in 1970

The die-hard fans of evergreen Dev Anand might know about this rare, lesser-known venture featuring the inspiring actor; but for many young friends here, it should be fascinating to know that the one and only Dev Anand also featured in a Hollywood film along with Zeenat Aman and Kieu Chinh, a leading lady from Vietnam, in the year 1970. Though reportedly Zeenat was already signed for *Hare Rama Hare Krishna* (1971), Dev chose her to feature in this English film as one of his leading ladies, maybe as a trial to see her presence on the silver screen. So, before the cult *Hare Rama Hare Krishna*, Dev Anand and Zeenat together appeared in this foreign venture not released for Indian viewers in that era for some dubious reasons.

Revealing the details about the film, it was a crime-thriller-cum-melodrama titled *The Evil Within*, a 20th Century Fox production, written as well as produced by Rolf Bayer and directed by Lamberto V. Avellana. Originally an English-language film, it was later also dubbed and released in Filipino (as a Philippines movie). Alternatively titled *Passport To Danger*, it introduced American actor Rod Perry in a key role (who also sang the theme song) along with Indian actors Prem Nath, Iftekhar, Jagdish Raj, Vimal Ahuja, Vipin Gupta, Shetty and more. Interestingly, the cinematographer of this Hollywood film was Fali Mistry, who was a close associate of Dev Anand in many of his films of that era, including *Guide* (1966).

Majorly shot in India around Jaipur and Udaipur's exotic locations (showcasing forts, deserts, mountains, camels, and more), the experimental 'James-Bond' kind of project revolving around the opium mafia wasn't an engrossing watch despite the dynamic presence of Dev Anand. So, while it was made to kick-start Dev's international career, it completely failed to do so as it largely went unnoticed abroad and therefore couldn't reach millions of fans in the actor's homeland too. As revealed by Dev in a TV interview, though the government had given permission to shoot the film in Rajasthan, still it was not allowed to be released in India by the Censor Board, due to its parallel track dealing with the controversial opium smuggling. Perhaps the lesbian angle in the film and bold kisses by Dev also had something to do with its censor issues.

Whatever the reason, the rare film eventually got lost in these avoidable controversies and did not get a formal release in India, thus remaining out of reach of Indian viewers who largely were not even aware of any such international project featuring Dev and Zeenat together. Thankfully, it has now been uploaded on YouTube and can easily be seen by all the true fans of the evergreen creator, Dev Anand, smartly dealing with international smugglers and their opium syndicate.

❖ ❖ ❖

Fact File: *The Evil Within* was conceived as a typical James Bond film with a similar format. It was earlier titled *Flower of Evil,* also *Inside Out* when it was being shot in India. A decade later, the original James Bond movie *Octopussy* (1983) was shot in similar locations in Udaipur as an intriguing coincidence.

Yash Johar, the founder of *Dharma Productions* and father of Karan Johar, worked as a production controller with the unit of *The Evil Within.*

CHAPTER TWELVE

SHOLAY'S FAMOUS WATER-TANK SEQUENCE AND ANTHONY QUINN

A lot has been already written, discussed, and discovered on various platforms about the epic creation *of Sholay* (1975) and all the backstage stories associated with its making. There have been numerous articles and a dedicated book too, written around the euphoria the film created in its year of release. And recently, many bloggers have also mentioned a lot about its evident sources of inspiration from world cinema, making some straight references.

Still, just when I thought probably everything had already been disclosed about the subject draining it completely, I incidentally got introduced to a scene from a Western classic, having huge similarities with the famous water-tank suicide sequence of *Sholay* featuring Dharmendra climbing up the tank to get his marriage with *Basanti* approved. It was reportedly based on a real-life instance of those times, but that doesn't seem to be the case when we witness an exactly similar sequence featuring in a foreign film, 6 years before the release of the Indian epic.

The scene features in the Oscar-nominated comic drama *The Secret of Santa Vittoria* released in the year 1969, directed by Stanley Kramer.

In the opening ten minutes of the film, we have its protagonist, Anthony Quinn, getting drunk and climbing up a big water tank with a liquor bottle in hand, scaring a huge crowd gathered on the ground wondering about the reason Quinn is up there. The people are waiting for him to come down safely and two ladies are watching it all from a distance, annoyingly cursing the man for his silly suicidal tendencies.

Now whether the sequence has something to do with a similar scene in Ramesh Sippy's milestone creation or not remains debatable, but there is no denying the fact that the two sequences do have many strange, striking similarities.

❖ ❖ ❖

Fact File: Amazingly I went through a similar kind of experience watching a train robbery sequence in an old English Classic *North West Frontier* (1959) directed by J. Lee. Thompson. The long sequence again has huge similarities with the famous train chase scene in the cult masterpiece *Sholay*, and the film has another Indian link as it features I. S. Johar, one of the most famous multifaceted personalities of our Hindi cinema playing a key role.

CHAPTER THIRTEEN

When Lata Mangeshkar, Mohd. Rafi, Kishore Kumar and Mukesh all sang together in one song

Hindi film lovers living all over the world are quite familiar with *Amar Akbar Anthony* (1977), one of the most famous entertainers from director Manmohan Desai, featuring three leading pairs of that time representing three different religions, as depicted in the film's title. The hit movie had some brilliant comic sequences between Amitabh Bachchan and Rishi Kapoor, plus had Vinod Khanna standing tall against Amitabh, his biggest competitor in the mid-'70s.

But apart from these popular merits, the film also had a rare occasion associated with a song in its melodious soundtrack. *Amar Akbar Anthony* is the only instance in the history of Hindi cinema wherein the four most respected stalwarts of our music industry sang together for the entire lead star cast of the film in a particular track.

The song was *Humko Tumse Ho Gaya Hai Pyar Kya Karein* in which Lata Mangeshkar, Mohd. Rafi, Kishore Kumar, and Mukesh all sang together for the first and last time, thereby creating history. Rafi sang for Rishi, Kishore for Amitabh, Mukesh for Vinod, and Lata for all three female actors – Shabana Azmi, Neetu Singh, and Parveen Babi (proving her supremacy).

Moreover, this particular song penned by Anand Bakshi also stood out in the entire soundtrack for its thoughtful musical arrangement, in which the composers Laxmikant-Pyarelal very insightfully incorporated the essence of all three religious communities depicted in the film, i.e., Hindu, Muslim, and Christian, uniquely and intelligently like never before.

Giving the ultimate creation its respectable due, just listen to the Western arrangements at the start of the song with all the strings and a choir singing in the interlude generating an 'Anthony' kind of impact. Then in the middle, the use of Duff gives the song an ethnic, traditional feel representing 'Amar' and later, the insertion of Qawwali beats with group claps perfectly suits 'Akbar' as the energetic lover.

No doubt, it is simply an outstanding achievement by the director, lyricist, music directors, singers, choreographers, and all the actors involved in the song representing a great creative team working together.

❖ ❖ ❖

Fact File: Four years later in Manoj Kumar's *Kranti* (1981), Laxmikant Pyarelal yet again came up with *'Chana Jor Garam'*, bringing together Lata Mangeshkar, Mohd. Rafi and Kishore Kumar in a song. But this time there was Nitin Mukesh, instead of his father accompanying the three maestros.

CHAPTER FOURTEEN

Balraj Sahni's inspiring speech at Delhi's Jawaharlal Nehru University in 1972

Reading articles in film magazines penned by renowned artists themselves and listening to their interviews before the '80s sharing a unique vision of life used to be an enriching experience, equivalent to going through some rich literature. The views expressed in those articles/interviews had many great insights to share that could also enlighten the reader about some relevant unknown truths about life, not exactly related to cinema.

Admittedly, I realised this fact while going through many old journals and other valuable stuff from that golden era and was literally taken aback seeing the amazing quality of thoughts shared by many industry veterans, like some revolutionary thinkers caring about the society they live in. One of those most important and must-read documents of them all happens to be the convocation speech by writer-thinker-social activist Balraj Sahni, the most natural actor of Hindi Cinema, speaking on his

1972 visit to the Jawaharlal Nehru University in Delhi. I am sure many of my friends reading it would feel pleasantly shocked knowing the vision of this immensely talented artist, who liked to say the truth as it is without any inhibitions and therefore is unanimously considered one of the most respected names of Hindi film industry.

Looking at the long document, many might try to avoid it thinking it is irrelevant or talking about something that might not be interesting enough. But for those friends, I would simply like to add that the long speech can certainly change your whole outlook towards the actors of that golden era and perhaps your whole perception about art, cinema, and society too.

So, to miss this would be a sin, if I may call it that, and if you still do not feel convinced, then do read this small excerpt taken from the long text and then decide on your own.

"Our little film world either offers the actor too little work, forcing him to eat his heart out in idleness; or gives him too much - so much that he gets cut off from all other currents of life. Not only does he sacrifice the pleasures of normal family life, but he also has to ignore his intellectual and spiritual needs.

In the last twenty-five years, I have worked in more than 125 films. In the same period, a contemporary European or American actor would have done thirty or thirty-five. From this, you can imagine what a large part of my life lies buried in strips of celluloid. A vast number of books which I should have read I have not been able to read. So many events I should have taken part in have passed me by. Sometimes I feel terribly left behind. And the frustration increases when I ask myself how many of these 125 films had anything significant in them. How many have any claim to be remembered? Perhaps a few; those could be counted on the fingers of one hand. And even those have either been forgotten already or will be, quite soon."

The more than 50-year-old speech is a well-known document for anyone knowing about the artist or the reputed university in Delhi, so much so that the enlightening address used to be printed and distributed by the JNU students' union at one point in time. Thankfully, the complete speech can be accessed online as uploaded by many reputed websites for the present and future generations to learn from.

So, if the above few lines look meaningful enough and worth your valuable time, then do search for the detailed text on the internet and have a good time reading and contemplating.

CHAPTER FIFTEEN

BOBBY AND ARCHIE COMICS

For friends who admire the works of the legendary showman Raj Kapoor, the facts related to RK Banner going through an extremely tough time after the debacle of *Mera Naam Joker* are quite well known. Plus, the way Raj Kapoor bounced back with his youthful project *Bobby* in 1973 is also widely known to every true lover of Hindi Cinema all over the globe.

However, an interesting piece of information that might not be known to many is that at the time of the release of this youthful trendsetter, its reputed writer K. A. Abbas also released a book/novel based on his original screenplay in English, aptly titled *Bobby - The Complete Story*. It was not a script published as it is, following the routine trend of those decades, but a complete English romantic novel (exactly on the lines of famous love series from *Mills & Boon)* that got duly appreciated by the young readers.

In the preface of the book, Abbas revealed that the novel has been published with only slight editing as it was written before any changes were made by the creative team in the later stages. He further added an interesting point elaborating on the same, saying that if studied with a comparative approach, it will give an insight into the creative process through which a filmmaker visualizes and transforms a story into his film on the screen.

In the introduction of the book's re-published version, Suresh Kohli mentions how the idea of a bubbly romantic story originated from the wide appreciation received by the opening section of *Mera Naam Joker* featuring Rishi Kapoor as the school kid. The thought was further consolidated when Raj Kapoor was once reading the famous comic book *Archie* (during the tough phase of his career), which was all about a group of youngsters having an interesting quote:

"Seventeen is no longer young; we have a life of our own too and we are aware of it."

The quote got stuck in the showman's mind and became the seed for his next film *Bobby.*

In a documentary made by the Films Division in the mid-1980s, the showman expressed, *"In a country like America, a young boy of seventeen said this sentence in an Archie comic book (spoken by Archie himself), and I think that is what caught me with the thought that here is something very big. It is profound. Today's children are not the same as they were 30 years back. They are much more aware of their environment and their knowledge. They are much more responsible than what 30-40 years back our forefathers were. They were grown-ups, they were married, they had children, and yet they were called, 'Chup Reh, Abhi Bachaa Hai Tu.' You cannot say this to a child today anymore."*

It was the debut film of Rishi Kapoor playing the young lover but was still titled *Bobby,* which happened to be the girl's name in the film – showcasing its director's strong conviction in his project. In other words, *Bobby* was actually Raj Kapoor's comeback film much more than Rishi Kapoor's debut, as accepted by Rishi himself.

Adding to the amazement, Kohli further states (as also mentioned in the Showman's *An Intimate Biography* by Bunny Reuben) that a particular girl was the contender for the lead role in *Bobby* much before Dimple Kapadia auditioned eliminating everyone else. That girl was none other than Neetu Singh, who after a few years went on to become Mrs. Rishi Kapoor.

❖ ❖ ❖

Fact File: An English novel on Raj Kapoor's mega biographical project *Mera Naam Joker* written by K.A. Abbas was also released by *Hind Pocket Books* in 1970, with its opening page saying *'To THE JOKER who lived within the heart of Raj Kapoor'*.

And then both the original novels of *Bobby* and *Mera Naam Joker* were re-published by Harper Collins in the year 2012 and 2014 respectively.

CHAPTER SIXTEEN

THE STORY BEHIND HMV LOGO AND THE ADORABLE DOG

Music company *HMV's* (His Master's Voice) logo featuring a phonograph and a dog staring at it is one of the most iconic logos designed to date. The image is not only familiar to every music lover but also easily recognized even by people who are remotely related to music or are not regular listeners. Interestingly, the logo has a true loving story related to its origin and the artist *Francis Barraud*, who painted it towards the end of the nineteenth century after getting inspired by his surroundings.

Francis's brother Mark had a fox terrier dog called *Nipper* who was very attached to his master and had a great bond with him. Unfortunately, Mark died and *Nipper* went on to live with Francis who used to paint regularly with *Nipper* sitting by his side.

Once, while some music was being played on a phonograph in Francis's room, the artist noticed *Nipper* listening to the notes very carefully and looking into the cylindrical speaker of the phonograph with surprise. While some writers say that those were the recordings of Mark which Francis got as his inheritance along with the phonograph, others are not sure whether it was Mark speaking through those recordings or not.

Anyhow, Francis found *Nipper* hooked to the phonograph with deep interest and that is when he decided to paint this scene, giving the title *His Master's Voice* to the painting. In a few places, though, it is also mentioned that Francis painted this after the death of *Nipper*. But whatever the case, it was *Nipper*, his master Mark, and the phonograph which in reality became the basic inspiration for Francis to give birth to this historical painting.

Next, assuming that this might interest the phonograph manufacturing companies of those days, the artist took the painting to a few of them but surprisingly it generated no interest and remained unsold till 1899 when *The Gramophone Company* bought it with a vision. They later adapted the same as their official trademark with an addition of one of their disc machines representing the company. After a few years, when it became hugely popular, they even named the company after the title of the painting, i.e., *HMV* (in abbreviated form) as part of their branding strategy that worked big time.

So, this is the actual story behind that loyal dog *Nipper* in the world-famous logo, looking at the phonograph, probably listening to *His Master's Voice*.

CHAPTER SEVENTEEN

DON AND ITS CULT SONG *KHAIKE PAAN BANARAS WALA*

The concept of swapping a character with his lookalike was featured in quite a few projects before the late '70s, like in *Salaam Mem Saab* (1961), *Mr. India* (1961), *Bombay Ka Chor* (1962), *China Town* (1962), *Sachaa Jhutha* (1970) and *Kalicharan* (1976). Yet, one film that stands out in its execution of this exciting plot is Chandra Barot's *Don* released in 1978. Ironically, its director could only make this one masterpiece alone in his entire career (with another dud and a few shelved projects), which still turned out to be a major trendsetter in terms of treatment, music, and performances along with several amusing anecdotes about its making for the enthusiastic movie buffs to savour.

Among these astonishing backstage stories is the one related to its hit song *'Khaike Paan Banaras Wala'* (composed by Kalyanji Anandji and penned by Anjaan), which to date remains the landmark feature of the film, with Amitabh Bachchan and Zeenat Aman dancing on the *dholak* beats showcasing their Indian moves.

To begin with, the said song was not even part of the film when it was shown to some of the famous personalities of that era, including Manoj Kumar. The track was added later (as per his suggestion) when it was felt that the film's narration was going too fast with all the chase and thrilling sequences coming one after the other, and some kind of relief or calming effect was needed to ease it out. Hence, to tone down the tension on screen, the song was inserted creating a whole new situation post-interval to bring in the much-desired balance, which indeed worked superbly for the film. However, at the time of its late addition, no one would have ever imagined the kind of history it would create after the film's release.

Secondly, when this upbeat song was being recorded in the studio by the inimitable Kishore Kumar, then, as the legendary singer was known, he actually demanded some *paans* in the studio itself before singing. He chewed them, spat on a sheet spread on the floor, and then sang the verses with the natural effects of the act as it is. So, the sounds of *paan* chewing and spitting that you hear in the track are all real.

Lastly, the other worth-mentioning truth related to the film's shooting schedule is that before beginning the song shoot, Amitabh was made to eat more than 15-16 *paans* to have a real red effect on his lips. The effect did come as desired but due to the *choona* in those *paans*, Amitabh burnt his lips and remained in pain for several days.

More than a decade later, Amitabh revealed in an interview that while conceiving the paan-chewing character and his mannerisms in *Don*, the immediate reference that came to his mind was of Dr. Rahi Masoom Reza, whom he had observed several times while working together in the films of Hrishikesh Mukherjee.

Concluding the write-up, it is said that this particular track was actually written and composed for Dev Anand's *Banarasi*

Babu released in 1973. Whether the story is true or not, destiny had a major role to play behind its insertion in *Don*, and the song is rightly considered as one of the most famous dancing tracks of Amitabh Bachchan and the Hindi film music of the '70s.

❖ ❖ ❖

Fact File: If you truly love the film and its pulsating background score, then just explore the theme music of *Together Brothers* (1974) by Barry White and find where you hear something exactly similar in *Don.*

CHAPTER EIGHTEEN

NEECHA NAGAR – THE FIRST INDIAN FILM TO WIN AT CANNES

Cannes Film Festival has been the talk of the town in recent years and it is loudly publicized as a great achievement for a film to feature there in any specific category. The festival is said to be considering Indian films more seriously now with many path-breaking and innovative film-makers strongly making their presence felt like never before.

But not many know about this remarkably proud fact that the inaugural Cannes Film Festival witnessed a classic Indian film not only participating but also winning their prestigious Grand Prix Award (now called The Palme d'Or/Golden Palm) for the *Best Film* in the year 1946, along with other winners including David Lean's *Brief Encounter.* So, it was long before the other pioneers of Indian cinema, like Satyajit Ray and Bimal Roy, impressed and won over the Western film-makers that an Indian Film went on to win such high-profile laurels in a reputed international festival, standing tall amongst the pioneers of the world cinema.

This proud cinematic achievement for India discussed above is credited to *Neecha Nagar* which talked about the social divide in the country even before independence and was also the debut film of one of the most gifted, inventive, and yet under-rated directors of India, Chetan Anand.

In those last years before India's independence, there were several restrictions over the creative expression in films, especially on the ones talking about any social reform or revolt. But being an active member of IPTA (Indian People's Theatre Association) and owner of many revolutionary ideas, Chetan Anand went on to make this 'true masterpiece' with the help of his group of friends on a strictly restricted budget. The reference to its initial days of conception is also there in the renowned actor Balraj Sahni's autobiography *Meri Filmi Aatamkatha* (as both Balraj and Chetan were good friends), wherein due to the government restrictions they even faced a shortage of raw stock but somehow managed to overcome the problem with mutual efforts.

Well-known actress Kamini Kaushal made her debut in it as the leading female character along with Rafiq Anwar, Uma Anand, Hameed Butt, Zohra Saigal and more. Since it was the era of music, songs, and melodrama, the film also featured some songs and dance sequences that were very intelligently edited out selectively in the print sent to Cannes (a slide at the beginning of the film clearly states that). Despite these songs and dances, it remains one of the most progressive, realistic, and visionary films made in India, which was rightly rated to be 'Ahead of its times' by many critics. As an additional lesser-known fact, *Neecha Nagar* was also the first film for which world-famous sitarist Pt. Ravi Shankar scored the music, before composing for many trendsetting films of Satyajit Ray.

But as it has always been the fate of such futuristic films, the authorities (before independence) did not allow it to be officially released in the country and the film kept waiting to reach its own audience for years. So, a shining product, which was constantly winning 'rare appreciation' abroad, was unfortunately not available to its countrymen, and with the passing years, the film's prints too got damaged and were even reported lost at one point in time. Later, after more than a decade, one of the prints was thankfully recovered, saving the country from a great loss. The print was then used to make the presently available (poor quality) video versions of the classic for the Indian audience.

The film is said to be inspired by the play *Lower Depths* by the Russian writer Maxim Gorky. But here the inspiration or similarity was more due to the similar social divide existing in most of the countries at that time, eventually leading to many identical conclusions. And it was this universal applicability of the film that in turn made it an important international project and one of the most memorable pre-independence works by an Indian director.

Surprisingly, and shamefully too, the story of *Neecha Nagar* openly reveals the so-called progress made by the country since the last century, as one can easily relate to its basic plot even today. In simple words, if I narrate to you a script that talks about a powerful rich landowner who, through his strong political connections, gets a sewage system approved, running right through a village situated on a lower land, then you are not going to find anything archaic in it at all. That is because, sadly, we still get to read many similar scams in newspapers talking about some remote areas and even cities dealing with identical problems in routine.

Neecha Nagar thoughtfully talks about this subject, which further crosses all moral boundaries, when the execution of the sewage project results in a contaminated water supply to the village and there is a near-epidemic leading to loss of lives. Shockingly the authorities take advantage of this grave situation too by hurriedly building up a hospital to take care of the victims 'free of cost,' posing as their only human saviour to depend upon.

With such a hard-hitting, socially relevant, and realistic script depicting the ugly plight of poor Indian villagers, the film was bound to get noticed both in the country as well as abroad. Apart from its burning subject, the film brought forward a legendary director at work through his interesting use of images, creative montage, and expressive shots that differentiated the film from many in the same genre being made all around the globe. In fact, the maturity with which Chetan uses the camera movements, dialogues, silence, and music in his various scenes makes it hard to believe that this was the first film of the veteran director in the mid-1940s.

Having said that, today it is surely going to be a tough watch for the younger generation as it requires a great amount of patience and passion to grasp the real essence behind all those superbly directed sequences by the maestro. Yet for ones who truly wish to experience such precious Indian gems appreciated by the world almost a decade before Ray's *Pather Panchali*, the film surprises as well as impresses, making a solid impact. That is the reason why *Neecha Nagar* continues to enjoy huge respect in the history of Indian cinema to date, though many youngsters might not have even heard about it.

Interestingly, the film also showcases another creative idea introduced by Chetan, wherein he did not use the word 'Director' in the credits of the film, but wrote 'Film Creation' along with his name, rightly indicating the history he was going to create in the later years of his career through many other gems.

Ending with an unfortunate fact about this important classic, *Neecha Nagar* can easily be called a priceless masterpiece that could not be released in its own country in the year of its making and remains a lesser-known or forgotten gem in a nation that is known around the world to cherish cinema the most.

Such is the ignorance towards this rare classic that for a long time, the original poster of the film was not available over the internet and only the one made by its home video company for their VCD Sleeves was in circulation.

With the hope that we soon realize the importance of saving and restoring our rich heritage for the coming generations, may this write-up inspire young friends to find some time and courage to watch this visionary classic and witness the excellence achieved by Indian Cinema way back in 1946.

❖ ❖ ❖

Fact File: As the film was winning appreciation all over in 1946, a letter was sent to Chetan Anand by an aspiring filmmaker in Calcutta, saying that the film inspired him to continue the struggle of making his first film and not lose hope. That letter was signed by Satyajit Ray.

According to a few unconfirmed reports, Shekhar Kapoor's much-publicized but jinxed project *Paani* is based on a subject quite close to the one we get to see in *Neecha Nagar*. That truly reveals how important and relevant the film is, even after seven decades of its making, post-independence.

Incidentally, Shekhar Kapoor is also the nephew of the Anand brothers and hence might be willing to revive the golden classic of his uncle, taking the family legacy forward.

CHAPTER NINETEEN

Ustad Nusrat Fateh Ali Khan's introduction in Hindi cinema

If a young student of today's new-age generation loves music but is still not familiar with the legendary name of *Ustad Nusrat Fateh Ali Khan,* then he has yet to experience a whole different world of music, capable of transporting its listeners to trance with blissful ease. His incomparable works continue to infuse new life into our otherwise routine schedules and his musical gems would surely be an inspiration for many generations to come in the times ahead.

Frankly talking about the master, his talented team, and his valuable associations with all the foreign artists, including Bally Sagoo, Peter Gabriel, Eddie Vedder, and our own Lata Mangeshkar, A. R. Rahman and many more, requires a whole chapter entirely devoted to their immortal creations. Therefore, here I would just like to focus on those early years when Ustad Nusrat Fateh Ali Khan was introduced to the film world of Mumbai, then called Bombay.

Gaining more popularity in India post the avoidable controversy in 1994 around the hit (inspired) track *Tu Cheez Badi Hai Mast Mast* from *Mohra,* which was a rehashed version of his devotional song *Dum Mast Qalander Mast Mast*, many assume the maestro entered the Indian musical scene in the mid-90s with Shekhar Kapoor's *Bandit Queen* (1994).

However, the fact remains that it was music director Khayyam who introduced Nusrat more than a decade back in 1981 in his film *Nakhuda* with the track *Haq Ali Ali* giving the credits as 'Nusrat Ali and Mujahad Ali'. The film was directed by Dilip Naik and was produced by another magician of his art, Yash Chopra.

Two years later, Nusrat could also be seen singing another devotional qawwali *Yaad Unki Rahey Dil Mein* on the screen making a special appearance in *Bismillah Ki Barkat* (1983) directed by K. Sharif.

But amazingly, even before these films, another musical genius invited Nusrat and party to perform at his son's wedding who was none other than the showman Raj Kapoor and the young couple that got married was Rishi Kapoor and Neetu Singh in the year 1980. Plus, the precious musical gem the team prepared for their prestigious performance in India was supposedly "*Sanson Ki Maala Pe Simrun Main Pee Ka Naam*" which later inspired another Hindi film song in the late '90s.

So, this wedding event in 1980 had the first-ever show of Ustad Nusrat Fateh Ali Khan in India, in front of almost all the stalwarts of the Hindi film industry, who were simply left spellbound by his performance.

CHAPTER TWENTY

AMITABH BACHCHAN'S SUPREMO COMIC BOOK SERIES IN THE '80S

Comic lovers must have fond memories of a rare series that originated from the amalgamation of the world of comics and Hindi cinema in the early '80s. Those were the years when Amitabh Bachchan was the indisputable ruler of the Box Office and an innovative comic book series was introduced featuring the superstar as the life-saving superhero *Supremo*, which continued for almost two years.

For young friends who are not aware of this comic series, it was called *The Adventures of Amitabh Bachchan (Kissey Amitabh Ke* in Hindi), which had a new issue released every month both in Hindi and English with titles such as *The Lost Idol, The Imposter, Invasion, The Hijack, The Lost City, The Kidnap* and more.

The series had Amitabh featured as a famous actor (as in real life) who used to turn into *Supremo* whenever there was a serious crime committed or in the time of a crisis in the city. He did not have any gifted superpowers but did wear a smart body-hugging suit like other famous superheroes. He wore big glasses to hide his real identity and had two friends, *Vijay* and *Anthony* (named after Amitabh's famous film characters), who shared the secret of his hidden persona and contributed to *Supremo's* various missions. Inspired by the immensely popular film *Coolie* (1983), the superhero also had a falcon *Shaheen*, that always informed Amitabh about the time to become *Supremo,* and a friendly whale *Sonali* guarding the island he owned.

The project was planned and released with Amitabh's approval and each edition featured a personally signed letter from him on the first page to greet the kids. The whole idea was conceived by Pammi Bakshi, then the editor of *Movie* magazine, who also got the famous director-poet-writer-lyricist Gulzar on board as a script consultant for the *Supremo* series. The books were published by *India Book House Pvt. Ltd.* (IBH) in *Star Comics* and its art department was headed by Pratap Mullick who was an illustrator for the *Amar Chitra Katha* books at that time.

Apart from showcasing directors like Manmohan Desai and Gulzar shooting their films with Amitabh, the comic series had another filmy connection as the name *Supremo* was actually picked from the sets of Amitabh-Randhir Kapoor film *Pukar* shot in Goa. During that shooting whenever Amitabh came on the set, the whole crowd watching the shoot used to become standstill. Seeing this, Randhir always said, *"Supremo has arrived."* Pammi Bakshi heard the name, liked it, and got an okay from Amitabh for the comic book series. That is how *Supremo* came to life.

The impact of this series was so huge that *Manoj Comics* also started its own version of books introducing an Amitabh-like character and a few other publications began a new series featuring some of the famous cricket stars (after the World Cup win in 1983), including Sunil Gavaskar as a detective. Plus, the trend was reportedly followed in the South too, turning lead actors into comic heroes around the same time.

Sadly, the series was discontinued by its publishing house after two years for undisclosed reasons, which disappointed kids and fans both in those particular years. Unfortunately, I also misplaced my personal collection of these issues but recently felt overjoyed again when I found the scans of a few of them thankfully uploaded on the net by some like-minded friends.

Anyhow, this rare comic series based on a superstar is clear proof that in those gone years not only the readers (both children and adults) but also the creators were so passionate about films that they loved to try innovative means of satisfying their artistic urge without even thinking about any big returns. Today, probably the excitement is still there as a few comic books have recently been released based upon specific film characters like *Krrish, Agent Vinod*, and more. But they were all part of the film's promotional campaign planned around the release, only to be discontinued later due to the time, effort, and money involved. Perhaps the change in times has made us all blind or so scared that we are not willing to try such innovations unless assured of some reasonable risk-free profits in return.

Luckily the new age gift of the worldwide web has once again enabled us to re-live our passion with these rare comics, albeit in the form of JPEG or PDF files saved on our computer hard drives. So thankfully, all is not lost yet!

CHAPTER TWENTY ONE

THE LAST JURY TRIAL IN INDIA AND THREE HINDI FILMS BASED ON IT

While watching many Western courtroom dramas, you might wonder looking at the *Jury* sitting in the court, as that is not the procedure followed by the Indian courts in the present. However, it was not the case more than half a century ago as *The Jury* prominently used to be a part of our judicial system too, giving their mutual verdict on cases based on the majority of votes. The intriguing *Nanavati* case of 1959 in Maharashtra was the last case involving a jury verdict before the system was withdrawn.

The case was about a naval officer murdering his long-time friend, a rich well-known person from the elite social circle having an illicit affair with the officer's wife. The verdict in the case became a milestone when the jury declared the accused 'not guilty' and the trial judge referred the case to the High Court after feeling that the jury was somehow not able to do justice or was misled.

The news of the case being referred to the Bombay High Court became the talk of the town wherein the accused finally got life imprisonment for the murder and then the Supreme Court also upheld HC's verdict later. However, after all the public agitation and media buzz, the Indian government granted a pardon to *Nanavati* in 1960, following which he left the country to settle abroad. Studying this particular case and its questionable initial verdict influenced by various reasons, the jury trials were abolished in India in 1960.

The case became an inspiration for a few books and three major Hindi films made in different eras.

1. Yeh Raaste Hain Pyar Ke / Love & Passion (1963)

The debut production of actor-producer-director Sunil Dutt (under the banner of Ajanta Arts), the film was directed by R. K. Nayyar and featured Sunil Dutt, Leela Naidu, Rehman, Ashok Kumar, and Moti Lal in the lead roles. Though it begins with a disclaimer that it is all based on fictitious characters and also has a filmy climax quite different from what happened in the famous case, still its real inspirational source was widely known. Hence, the film's courtroom scenes were of immense importance, brilliantly enacted by both Ashok Kumar and Moti Lal playing the two lawyers.

Apart from being a tense courtroom drama, it also had some great memorable songs composed by Ravi and penned by Rajendra Krishan, like *Rooh Khatam Ho Gayi, Tum Jispe Nazar Dalo,* and more. In fact, the film begins with three back-to-back songs in the first 15 minutes and then cuts to the courtroom scenes as per the script's basic requirement. Another truth about this courageous effort is that it did not work in many of the major centers and could impress only a certain section of the viewers in some metro cities.

2. Achanak (1973)

After a decade post *Yeh Raaste Hain Pyar Ke*, the renowned poet-writer-lyricist-director Gulzar made a different, experimental film on the same subject which was more a story of love and betrayal instead of a courtroom drama. The film was based on the story of K.A. Abbas, titled *13th Victim.*

In actual terms, the proceedings of *the Nanavati* case form only the basic plot of *Achanak*, and the film mostly revolves around the main protagonist's army-training scenes, his days spent in a hospital, his running away from the police, and the chase sequences clubbed with the flashbacks of his past until the climax.

Featuring Vinod Khanna, Lily Chakravarty, Om Shivpuri, and Iftekhar in the lead roles, it does not have anything to do with the courts and was fairly accepted at the Box Office too as an emotional story of vengeance. Despite being a Gulzar film, it was a song-less venture with a background score by Vasant Desai but featured repeated use of '*Sun Mere Bandhu Re*' from *Sujata* in a few of its key sequences (in the backdrop).

3. Rustom (2016)

In comparative terms, though both the films mentioned above were majorly inspired by the *Nanavati* case, they still did not use the fact in their publicity campaign or posters, creating their own identity in the history of Hindi cinema.

On the other hand, Tinu Suresh Desai's *Rustom* released in 2016 prominently used the source matter in its well-planned promotional campaign, making it a proper news item. The tagline "*3 shots that shocked the nation*" used in its posters was in reality the headline of *Blitz* newspaper in 1959 with a slight change of words.

Produced by Neeraj Pandey, and featuring Akshay Kumar and Illeana D'Cruz in the lead, *Rustom* specifically focused on the court case and fictionalized the real happenings of those times presenting it as an engrossing crime thriller. It became a success at the box office and once again brought the decisive case into the limelight enlightening the new generation.

However, none of the three films clearly informed the viewers, what conclusive difference the case made in the Indian Judiciary, abolishing the jury system forever in the early '60s.

❖ ❖ ❖

Fact File: Hrishikesh Mukherjee also used *'Sun Mere Bandhu Re'* from *Sujata* in one of the key scenes of *Abhimaan* (played in the background). Maybe it was a humble tribute given by both Gulzar and Hrishikesh Mukherjee to their mentor Bimal Roy.

Towards the end of *Achanak*, one can also spot another famous song being played as an instrumental track in the background, which is *'Koi Hota Jisko Apna"* from Gulzar's directorial debut *Mere Apne.*

Post the OTT revolution in the country, the infamous Nanavati Case was again adapted for a crime mystery web series titled *The Verdict – State Vs Nanavati* in the year 2019.

CHAPTER TWENTY TWO

PAKEEZAH AND ONE OF ITS FAMOUS SONGS WITHOUT MEENA KUMARI

Pakeezah (1972), a magnum opus of poetic expressions on celluloid, remains as pure as its apt title, even in these progressive years of the twenty-first century. It still has the power to teleport you to those innocent years of the bygone era, when music, poetry, dance, and love were cherished as the most valuable possessions of a passionate person. Featuring the legendary tragedy queen *Meena Kumari,* the movie is considered an important milestone in the history of Hindi Cinema and enjoys cult status due to its out-of-the-world direction, poetic dialogues, realistic performances, and pure immortal music.

Incidentally, as it was destined to be, the film that was launched initially in the late '50s, took almost 14 years to shine in the theaters. In this long span of time, it witnessed several break-ups, separations, changes, and additions, which are still unknown to many film lovers all over the world. As a result, many lengthy essays and books too have been published on this unforgettable gem in recent years. The music company HMV later also released a rare album of all the unreleased tracks of the film titled *Rang-Barang*. The album had a tagline saying "Songs recorded for *Pakeezah* but not used in the film."

However, here I would like to mention an interesting fact, which is there to be seen in the film itself and is not just another 'behind-the-curtain' information to make you feel nostalgic.

As the shooting of *Pakeezah* resumed in the late '60s, Meena Kumari was suffering from a critical health condition and was under observation. But since she was always Amrohi's only choice, she agreed to complete the film as a thorough professional after a timely intervention of Sunil Dutt & Nargis, despite her known differences with Amrohi and severe illness. Still, Meena Kumari's health issues required that some of the dance sequences and scenes be shot without her. So, while Amrohi reportedly took the long shots using a double in a few of the dance sequences (with Padma Khanna as it is stated), he actually shot the entire song sequence of *Chalo Dildaar Chalo, Chaand Ke Paar Chalo* without showing Meena Kumari's face even once.

Now do see the melodious song yet again and witness how the director played with the dark ambience and various shots of the moon, sky, stars, the boat in the river, and more without showing even a glimpse of his heroine's face in the complete song sequence in an intelligent manner, post one initial shot of the couple.

Sadly, Meena Kumari died just a few weeks after the film was released. Till then, the movie was having a lukewarm response at the box office. But as the news of her death spread, the project unintentionally got associated with her sudden demise and started getting huge appreciation from the viewers. Later it was declared a hit, acquiring a cult status in the history of Indian cinema as Meena Kumari's swan song.

❖ ❖ ❖

Fact File: It is ironic that Meena Kumari's actual last release was Sawan Kumar Tak's directorial debut *Gomti Ke Kinare* in 1972, which surprisingly failed miserably at the box office. It had music by R.D. Burman and lyrics by Majrooh Sultanpuri.

CHAPTER TWENTY THREE

KOMAGATA MARU TRAGEDY IN 1914 AND JEEVAN SANGRAM

Looking back at the unfortunate incident of 1914, the Canadian government issued a commemorative stamp in May 2014, the centenary year of the tragedy, respectfully remembering the more than 350 Indians who became victims of this horrific event.

Two years later in May 2016, Canada's Prime Minister Justin Trudeau formally apologized in the House of Commons for the Komagata Maru incident of 1914, in which hundreds of Sikhs, Muslims, and Hindu passengers were denied entry to Canada and sent back to meet their uncertain fate in India.

On the other hand, it is quite sad that the incident is not even known or remembered with equal respect by the citizens of our own country, not even by the people of Punjab. So, this is my humble attempt to enlighten all young friends about that heartbreaking event of 1914 and a Hindi film made on the same released way back in 1974.

About the actual incident

Komagata Maru was a Japanese steamship hired by an influential Sikh, Baba Gurdit Singh, sailing towards Canada with 376 Indians aboard, including 340 Sikhs, 24 Muslims, and 12 Hindus as per the history books. The ship reached Vancouver on May 23, 1914, but due to certain migration restrictions, its passengers were not allowed to get off and only 20 of the 376 people were given permission, after proving their resident status.

The ship was then sent back to India and it reached a port near Calcutta after a long, tiring voyage towards the end of September (after four months). But shockingly, here several travellers of the ship were gunned down by the British troops near *Baj Baj Ghat*, only a few managed to escape, whereas the rest were all imprisoned in their own country under the British Raj. This tragedy was one of the major historical events of the early 20th century, hugely contributing towards triggering India's freedom struggle over the next three decades.

A rare Hindi film made on Komagata Maru

Dedicating the project to Baba Gurdit Singh, writer-producer-director Rajbans Khanna made a spirited Hindi film titled *Jeevan Sangram* in the year 1974, which, instead of showcasing the whole journey, was a fictional account of the events happening after the ship returned to India. The movie featured Shashi Kapoor, Radha Saluja, Om Shiv Puri, Iftekhar, Murad, Asit Sen, Jalal Agha, Manmohan, Tarun Bose, Padma Khanna, Tuntun and many more in key roles of revolutionary Indians and had its soundtrack composed by Kalyanji-Anandji. The songs had melodious voices of Lata Mangeshkar, Asha Bhosle, Usha Mangeshkar, Mahendra Kapoor, and Narender Chanchal, singing the lyrics of Indivar, M. G. Hashmat and Gulzar. The screenplay and dialogues were also written by Gulzar and Qamar Jalalabadi, which undoubtedly gave the project a finer edge.

Made with a very authentic feel of Punjab, the film had some thoughtfully written dialogues in its well-executed climax, mentioning the teachings of Jesus Christ and the huge sacrifice of the entire family and the four young sons of the tenth Guru of the *Sikhs*, Guru Gobind Singh.

Unfortunately, *Jeevan Sangram* remains one of those forgotten but visionary films made in the '70s on India's independence movement. Plus, the *Komagata Maru* incident is still sadly not known to a big proportion of our population, which remains an important reason why this lesser-known film needs to be seen and introduced to the present generation as a must.

❖ ❖ ❖

Fact File: Over the last decade, repeated announcements have been made for a project based on the historical event to be directed by Deepa Mehta with a probable cast featuring Amitabh Bachchan, Akshay Kumar, and other international artists. But sadly, the project has not taken off yet.

CHAPTER TWENTY FOUR

CINEMA CINEMA AND FILM HI FILM - TWO UNIQUE ATTEMPTS BEFORE THE '90S

Celebrating the hundred years of Indian cinema, this chapter informs about two unusual and lesser-known film projects having some exclusive inclusions, which might interest the ardent lovers of Hindi cinema and its legendary artists.

Cinema Cinema (1979)

Produced and directed by Krishna Shah (of *Shalimar* fame), this interestingly conceived project was made in the late '70s following a novel and futuristic vision. Actually, it is not a film with any routine storyline but a kind of docu-drama in which a movie is running at a local single-screen theater and people from all walks of life are watching it, giving their personal remarks and comments. In other words, it is an account of a 'Live audience' enjoying a Hindi film in a theater in their normal routine life.

But here, as an appealing fact, the movie running on the screen (in the film), also happens to be a documentary featuring four superstars of that era enlightening the viewers about the history of Indian cinema commencing from the year 1913. So, we have Hema Malini, Amitabh Bachchan, Dharmendra, and Zeenat Aman sharing some valuable insights with the viewers as anchors.

Director Krishna Shah reportedly compiled this documentary on Indian cinema after his extensive research on the film archives available all over the world. Hence the project has footage from many officially released films from the beginning of the 20th century to the 1970s. Editing a quite engaging sequence of these distinctive clips, Shah explains the various schools of filmmaking and the historical progression of Indian cinema starting from its initial years of silent films. Therefore, the project and its content certainly can be rated as a first-of-its-kind attempt for Indian viewers.

Writer, Producer, Director: Krishna Shah

Starring: All the leading stars of the '70s, including Amitabh Bachchan, Dharmendra, Hema Malini, Zeenat Aman, Kim and many more.

Film Hi Film (1983)

An amateur but unique kind of movie, this is an even more interesting project incorporating all the unseen clips and unused songs of certain films that either did not find any takers or got stalled/shelved due to various reasons. *Film Hi Film* was made in 1983 and revolves around the story of a producer (played by Pran) who attempts to complete a film of all newcomers with a mere fifty thousand rupees. In the process, he faces many obstacles but leaves no stone unturned and takes those hurdles as a challenge to finally release the film in the theaters. Playing an unusual trick, *Film Hi Film* has several unrelated sequences and songs deliberately incorporated into the script, which actually are some partial scenes or tracks taken from all shelved films.

In clear words, this can easily be called a messy collage of clips taken from several movies that could not somehow make it to the screen. The scenes range from good to below average, which probably might have been the reason why they were not used in the projects planned by their reputed makers.

As mentioned in the opening credits, the films from which these unseen footages were taken include *Behrupiya* (1964), *Khuda Gawah* (1970), *Reporter* (1960), *Naya Mandir* (1961), *Shikwah* (1954), *Jahan Mile Dharti Aakash* (1962), *Sajan Ki Galiyan* (1968), *Sasta Khoon Mehnga Pani* (1964), *Ek Tha Chander Ek Thi Sudha* (1970), *Picnic* (1960) and *Yeh Basti Yeh Log* (1958).

Plus, the scenes incorporated in the movie feature many legendary artists like:

1. Raj Kapoor in a newspaper office getting arrested after making some weird predictions.
2. A complete song *Tauba Tauba* featuring Amitabh Bachchan and Rekha. (The song was in reality shot for a film titled *Duniya Ka Mela* (not mentioned in the credits). But later Amitabh was replaced by Sanjay Khan for some undisclosed reasons, resulting in two versions of the song.)
3. Amitabh's fight scene in a double role, with one wearing a veil and a cowboy hat and the other with a red scarf around his neck (dubbed in a different voice).
4. Another song, *Kitna Rangeen Hai*, featuring Guru Dutt and Sadhna singing on the deck of a ship.
5. Raj Kapoor as a Joker performing on stage, singing a fine track – *Has Kar Hasa, Masti Mein Ga, Kal Hoga Kya, Bhool Ja Bhool Ja* – long before playing the iconic role of a Joker in his biographic epic *Mera Naam Joker*.

6. Another sequence of Raj Kapoor in the same newspaper office followed by a scene with 'a talking dog'.
7. Manoj Kumar and Mala Sinha's family confronting sequence.
8. A complete song, *Suno Aye Duniya Walon,* featuring Manoj Kumar and Mehmood.
9. Raj Kumar teaching the heroine how to use a gun and revealing a hidden truth.
10. Dilip Kumar talking about a ceasefire on the war front and facing a court martial along with an emotional scene featuring Nutan.
11. Mehmood posing as a modern lady.
12. Dev Anand and Sadhna in a romantic scene and song, *Hum Khoob Jaantey Hain Kya Dil Mein Hai Tumhare,* along with Zaheeda.
13. Helen singing a short version of a club dance number, *Aadmi Ko Jeena Hai,* with Guru Dutt watching her in style.
14. Madhubala singing another short song, *Idhar To Dekho* in a hotel as Balraj Sahni watches in the get-up of a villager.
15. Vyjayanthimala performing on an instrumental track at a big set.
16. Rekha singing the *mukhda* of a song *Lambi Lambi Kaali Raatein* in an Arabian set-up.
17. Clipping of a well-shot police-dacoits encounter from K. Asif's unfinished venture *Sasta Khoon Mehnga Paani* as told by Pran in the film itself.
18. Rajendra Kumar saving a girl from the dacoits and fighting using his Shoe as a weapon.

Randomly including all the above clips, the film keeps returning to the story of that poor producer, who in the end, somehow manages to complete the venture. The film eventually becomes a big hit after getting released, cracking a satirical joke on the entire questionable system and its so-called creativity.

Produced By: Shahab Ahmed
Directed By: Hiren Nag
Starring: Pran, Ramesh Deo, Seema Deo, and more.
Music: Bappi Lahiri
Lyrics: Indivar

In conclusion, no doubt the above two ventures have a unique concept and presentation along with limitations of the budget. Yet they still need to be seen at least once, especially for all those unseen and rare sequences featuring many of our favourite stars.

CHAPTER TWENTY FIVE

JAGJIT SINGH'S CAMEO IN AMAN IN HIS ORIGINAL PERSONA WITH A TURBAN

As many might be feeling surprised or pleasantly shocked reading the heading here, frankly I was also in the same state when I first came to know about this rare fact accidentally. It was while researching the only movie appearance of Noble Award winner Bertrand Russell in the 1967 Hindi film *Aman* (made on world peace/also mentioned in another chapter of the book) that I got stuck on a particular scene, in which Rajendra Kumar celebrates his final medical exam results with his college friends.

One of those friends in the scene was a smart turbaned *Sikh* with a familiar face and voice. So I kept thinking about who he could be and then went back to the film's titles, having no mention of the supporting cast in the credits. On the other hand, the IMDB page of the movie did have a mention of that person and it was written Jagjit Singh as Rajendra's friend *(uncredited)*. Having worked with the maestro during the song recordings of the Punjabi film Sat Sri Akal (2008), it was truly a shocking but pleasant surprise for me as a die-hard fan, living in the misconception that I knew almost all about the genius and his earlier works.

However, still not believing the fact, I dug in more to confirm and was assured by friends close to Singh that the man was indeed the immensely gifted musical wizard, the master of soothing melodies and the elegant Ghazal exponent, in the only Hindi film cameo with his original persona of a *Sikh*.

So if you too wish to witness Jagjit Singh in this rare appearance, then do watch this unsung gem of the past made on world peace, aptly titled *Aman*. The sequence is right there at the beginning of the film when Rajendra Kumar successfully clears his medical degree and is being congratulated by a few of his college friends calling for a celebration.

CHAPTER TWENTY SIX

DISCO DANCER AND A FEW LITTLE-KNOWN FACTS ABOUT ITS CULT STATUS

Though on logical terms one can easily find many flaws and unexplainable situations in B. Subhash's superhit *Disco Dancer.* But the film certainly introduced a fresh, welcome change in the year 1982 becoming a cult phenomenon of its times surprising the trade pundits. It became an instant success at the box office, largely due to its hit music, Mithun Chakraborty's trademark dance movements, and a unique climax (never tried before or after) having three full-length songs played one after the other.

Further, as a known fact that may surprise many, it was also declared one of the top grossers of 1982, performing brilliantly along with major successful films such as *Namak Halaal, Khud-Daar, Nikaah, Prem Rog, Arth, Sanam Teri Kasam, Desh Premee, Satte Pe Satta* and Richard Attenborough's *Gandhi.*

More astonishingly, *Disco Dancer* is also one of the highest earners and among the five most famous films ever in Russia

(Soviet Union), standing tall along with gems such as *Awara, Shree 420, Seeta Aur Geeta,* and *Bobby.* Besides, there are several amazing anecdotes related to Mithun's unbelievable craze among Soviet citizens as *The Dancer* (including one about his statue called *Jimmy*) which even forced the Soviet press to invent a title for all Mithun fans as *Mithunists*. Its catchy hit numbers *'Jimmy Jimmy' (sung by Parvati Khan), 'I Am A Disco Dancer' (sung by Vijay),* and more composed by Bappi Lahiri and written by Anjaan are among the most favourite tracks performed as well as played during their major celebrations even today. Reportedly, post the film's release, people used to greet Indians in Russia as *"from the land of Disco Dancer,"* exactly like they did referring to *Awara* in the past.

However, like in India, the film did receive a few poor reviews in the Russian press as well when it was initially released. But such was the backlash to those reviews in the public letters received by various publications that it eventually resulted in quite a passionate debate in the film magazines at that time forcing the press to step back. Moreover, it was due to this unbelievable following of the film as well as its star Mithun that 26 years later in 2008, when writer Sudha Rajagopalan came up with her book on *Indian Cinema and Soviet Movie-Going After Stalin*, she also decided to name it as *Leave Disco Dancer Alone,* giving a clear indication of the film's undisputed cult status in that part of the world, not widely known in our country. As a matter of fact, *Disco Dancer's* craze was not just confined to Russia, as the film was equally loved in many other parts of the world too, including China, Africa, Israel, Japan, and more as stated by its director B. Subhash in one of his interviews.

As an interesting fact, Subhash announced this film while he was still shooting for *Taqdeer Ka Badshah* with Mithun. Knowing that Mithun was upset because his films were not doing well at the box office, he promised to give him a hit that would make him a big star, and he delivered on his promise, giving him *Disco Dancer*.

Apart from the director and the lead cast, one name that made a major contribution to *Disco Dancer's* amazing success in the country as well as overseas remains Bappi Lahiri. It is mainly because of his catchy music that the film is still being celebrated all over the world by its die-hard fans and its old original LPs are lapped up by music lovers at unbelievable prices.

Contradicting the above facts, in 2011, Harper Collins published a book on *Disco Dancer* with the tagline '*A Comedy in Five Acts*' by Anuvab Pal, strangely projecting it as a comic film with a touch of sarcasm. But many do refer to it as the worst film of the '80s despite its huge success.

Keeping in mind these conflicting viewpoints, I would humbly like to add that any creative expression like film needs to be studied and written upon in the context of its actual time of creation or release specifically. Otherwise, every generation will keep on making fun of its predecessors, which is not the way to study the past or, in this case, the Indian cinema.

CHAPTER TWENTY SEVEN

The common scene in Hrishikesh Mukherjee's GOLMAAL and JURMANA

Shooting simultaneously for two of his distinctive films in 1978-79, celebrated director Hrishikesh Mukherjee very intelligently incorporated one common scene in both *Golmaal* and *Jurmana,* which quite amazingly neither looked odd nor seemed to be forced in.

The basic scene is actually one of the very first sequences of *Jurmana*, in which Amitabh Bachchan plays a rich, spoilt Casanova and is flirting with a beautiful lady in a restaurant. The person sitting beside the lady objects to his indecent advances and gives Amitabh a solid punch for the same. In reply, Bachchan slowly comes back, reacting in his famous drunkard style to deliver the dialogue.

Now the same scene is there in *Golmaal* too in the form of an actual film shoot going on in a studio, where Deven Verma comes in with Amol Palekar. Here, at first, the director shows the viewers the complete scene being shot along with the same dialogues, and when Amitabh finishes the shoot, he greets both Deven and Amol, where Deven begins the conversation by saying:

"Hi Hero, Kis Ki Naukri Kar Raha Hai?"

"Haan Yaar.......Jurmana" – Amitabh replies.

"Abhi Tak Complete Nahin Hui?" Deven questions.

"Nahin Yaar" – comes the reply again and then after a casual introduction, Amitabh moves towards a group of school girls and starts giving autographs.

So, the same shot is used in two different films of the veteran director as it is. And that is indeed quite an interesting use of an opportunity available, merging both projects, probably being shot in the same studio at the same time, and that too with an amusing touch of reality by taking the viewers behind the camera.

In fact, it is this effortless creation and realistic simplicity for which Hrishikesh Mukherjee will always be remembered by the Hindi film audience in India as well as abroad.

CHAPTER TWENTY EIGHT

SURAHI – A GHAZAL ALBUM'S LOVABLE ASSOCIATION WITH MANOJ KUMAR AND RAJ KAPOOR

Ghazal is fast becoming an art form or genre of the gone era in this present age of the Internet. But speaking truthfully, I strongly feel that if one has not experienced, felt, and grasped the lovable essence of Urdu poetry in life, then he/she has truly missed the joy of one of the most blessed and precious treasures of existence offered to mankind.

The art was close to my heart from the early teens and as an ardent fan, I was always looking for new cassettes released in the Ghazals section since the mid-'80s. There were many memorable and landmark albums released by the world-renowned maestros in those 'Ghazal-loving times' before the cable TV revolution. But this exclusive write-up talks about one of those rare, forgotten, and lesser-known albums of the decade that remain amongst the best works I have ever heard by a debutant artist, even after almost four decades.

Probably many of the readers here might not have even heard of this album released in 1987, since neither the artist came up with any other attempt post his debut nor did the album get a deserving revival during the audio CD wave in the country after a few years of its release. Moreover, the Pop music industry, which was at its peak in the early '90s, turned out to be the last nail in the coffin for such exclusive albums that quickly went off the shelves without the much-needed support in the market.

Coming to the lifeline of the subject, this widely appreciated album was called *Surahi* and it featured 8 fabulous ghazals, simply, yet soulfully, sung by Vishal Goswami, son of the legendary filmmaker Manoj Kumar. The melodious compositions in the album were composed by the duo of Uttam Singh and Jagdish Khanna (then popularly known as Uttam-Jagdish) and the 8 touching ghazals penned by 5 renowned poets remain the favourites of many fans like myself, even after decades of reading poetry and listening to the new music.

Surahi was initially released by the *T-Series* music company in cassette form and audio CD format later in the 1990s. Along with its highly enjoyable tracks, the album had another unique feature which was a very rare and never-before inclusion for a ghazal album. It was a humble and loving introduction of Vishal by none other than the showman of the Hindi film industry, Raj Kapoor, which should undoubtedly be enough to prove the quality of work presented by the young artist.

But that is not all. One of those 8 ghazals, the title track *Surahi La Surahi,* was penned by the maestro Manoj Kumar himself and it had beautiful verses like:

"Bhatkega Har Gali Mein, Gham Ne Jo Mujhko Chhorha,
Torhegi Duniya Usko Bhi, Jaise Mujhko Torha"

So, if you are a true fan of the genre, then do try to get hold of this *Surahi* that has Raj Kapoor, Manoj Kumar, Uttam-Jagdish, and Vishal Goswami together pouring some exceptionally great ghazals dipped in melodious music.

CHAPTER TWENTY NINE

De De Pyar De from SHARAABI, Runa Laila and Bengali Music

Runa Laila, a famous playback singer in Bangladesh, Pakistan, and India, enjoyed a huge following in the musical corridors of these three neighbouring countries during the '70s and '80s, and amongst her immensely popular numbers in India were *Dama Dam Mast Qalander* and *Mera Babu Chhail Chhabila Main To Nachungi.*

She made an exciting debut in Hindi films in the early '70s and then worked with many renowned music directors such as Jaidev, Kalyanji Anandji, Laxmikant Pyarelal, and Bappi Lahiri. Her most famous Hindi film songs are the title song of *Ek Se Badh Kar Ek* (1976), *Do Dewaane Shehar Mein, Mujhe Pyar Tumse Nahin Hai* from *Gharonda* (1977), *Alibaba Mil Gaya Chaalis Choron Se* from *Agneepath* (1990) and more.

In 1982, Runa Laila released a private Pop album titled *Superuna* which was presented by Bappi Lahiri as the music director. One of the 10 tracks in the album was *De De Pyar De* which started with the line *Hum Bande Hain Pyar Ke, Maange*

Sabki Khair (penned by Anjaan). The song had exactly the same composition and music as later used in Prakash Mehra's *Sharaabi* released in 1984.

Interestingly, *Sharaabi* also had Bappi Lahiri as its music director and reportedly the track *De De Pyar De* was initially supposed to be sung by Runa Laila as informed to the singer then. But later, for some unknown reasons, it came out as an Asha Bhosle number in the film's original soundtrack and went on to become a major hit, with the male version sung by Kishore Kumar becoming an even bigger success.

Hence, as destiny had it, this famous track, which eventually went into the kitty of Asha Bhosle and Kishore Kumar, was originally Runa Laila's song from her private Pop album – the copyrights of which must have been with Bappi Lahiri himself as he was also the presenter of *Superuna* (clearly mentioned on the album sleeve).

But amazingly that is not all.

The basic composition of the track has Bangla folk in its roots, originally sung as "Allah Megh De" by Abbasuddin Ahmed from Bengal. The same was adapted as the popular *Allah Megh De* in Navketan's *Guide* (1966) composed by S. D. Burman.

CHAPTER THIRTY

THE ENIGMA AROUND THE MUSIC ALBUM LAL DUPATTA MALMAL KA IN 1989

There was a time when the music of a hit private album or film used to become a rage all over the country in just a few days of its release. It was an era when music cassettes used to sell like soft drinks in lakhs and music companies used to earn a fortune out of a single hot-selling album in just a few weeks.

One of these music companies operating in the country at that time was T-Series, which is still one of the leading ones in the present. Apart from the known allegations of piracy, the company was superbly led by the Late Gulshan Kumar who had a remarkable musical and business sense in the era when good music was evolving as an independent identity different from the usual film soundtracks in the market. In fact, T-Series was the only major company at that time as HMV (now *Saregama*) was struggling to maintain its existence in the market.

Gulshan Kumar and his team's fabulous musical instincts were repeatedly proved by how they capitalised on every great album coming their way and one of their truly melodious albums was

Lal Dupatta Malmal Ka in 1989. The music was first released as a private music album with songs written by Majrooh Sultanpuri and sung by Udit Narayan, Anuradha Paudwal, Suresh Wadkar, Pankaj Udhas, and Mohd. Aziz. The album had superb music by Anand Milind who had just tasted success with *Qayamat Se Qayamat Tak* and it included gems such as *Kya Kartey Thhey Saajna, Sooni Sooni Akhiyon Mein, Ab Dawa Ki Zaroorat Nahin, Tumne Rakh To Lee Tasveer Hamari* and more. I personally loved *Main Gul Hun Kali Hun Saba Hun* and listen to it even today, decades after the soundtrack's initial release.

Amazingly, the album became such a phenomenal success within a week of its release that there used to be constant repeat orders from the dealers almost daily. And I have a personal experience of this euphoria to recall as one of our friends then had a music shop in our locality and we used to constantly monitor the craze every single day.

At first, everyone was confused about what the album exactly was: a private music album, an original film soundtrack, a compilation, or something else. Probably that gave another brilliant idea to the company and they suddenly announced a telefilm coming soon in its new posters.

Perhaps this was the first ever video/telefilm that was creatively made in no time on a story revolving around its already famous songs that had become a countrywide craze in 1989. Next, within a few months of the announcement, the VHS tapes of the film were released, which once again were in demand due to the novel concept introduced by its courageous makers. The credits on its sleeve said, *Lal Dupatta Malmal Ka - A Romantic Film*, Directed by Ravinder Peepat. The film had Sahil Chadda as its hero and Viverly as the heroine along with other artists. As a telefilm shot in video format, it was never meant to be released on the big screen but surely was a stupendous success in both the audio and video market in that particular year.

Exactly similar hype was also seen the subsequent year when T-Series released another big musical hit titled *Aashiqui* in 1990. An identical confusion was there related to this album too in the beginning, as there was no hero or heroine shown on the cassette's sleeve and it had only a boy and a girl hiding under a coat. For a week or so, *Aashiqui* was also considered to be another telefilm made by the company, but this misconception was soon cleared by an official announcement mentioning all the credit details.

As a matter of fact, both the above-mentioned albums – *Lal Dupatta Malmal Ka* and *Aashiqui* – still hold the highest-selling album records for its company T-series.

Those were really the days when music albums were bought and played by the nation following a crazy passion. And fanatics like myself even used to buy another copy of the same album as a backup because many times the cassette used to entangle in the players and we had to buy a new one at once to stay hooked to our favourite music uninterrupted.

Somehow the passion has all vanished but the seven musical notes will always be there for the coming generations to feel the blessed ecstasy.

❖ ❖ ❖

Fact File: Such was the popularity of the video film and its songs in the audio-video market that T-Series came up with its sequel the very next year titled *Phir Lehraya Laal Dupatta Malmal Ka* in 1990. It cleverly explored the same songs and footage, in a plot revolving around reincarnation, also featuring Gulshan Kumar in a cameo as seen in the original film. Unfortunately, that did not work and the sequel could not win over the viewers in the same manner.

CHAPTER THIRTY ONE

AMITABH BACHCHAN, SUBHASH GHAI & THEIR DEVAA

One of the most successful and versatile actors in Hindi films, the legendary Amitabh Bachchan has worked with almost every renowned director in the industry. But have you ever thought why the once great showman Subhash Ghai never signed him, despite being one of the most sought-after directors of those times?

Actually, he did sign him for a film called *Devaa* in the late '80s, which got started with a grand muhurat as per the celebrated reputation of Subhash Ghai and his banner. However, due to some undisclosed reasons (mostly projected as ego clashes between the veterans), the project was shelved without any detailed announcement and could not, unfortunately, make it to the silver screen. Interestingly, in the muhurat shot of *Devaa,* Amitabh had a get-up very similar to the one later adapted in *Khuda Gawah.* With a mashaal in the hand, a long shining robe, and a turban minus the beard, the character looked exactly like the younger, thinner version of *Baadshah Khan* coming from Afghanistan. The similarity in the get-up was not appreciated by Ghai as revealed in one of his interviews of those times and he clearly called it 'unprofessional and unexpected.'

While we were lucky to see Amitabh in a similar-looking get-up used brilliantly by Mukul S. Anand making his own required additions in *Khuda Gawah* released in 1992, sadly the two giants of Indian cinema could never reconsider the project sorting their issues out. As a result, we missed the golden opportunity of seeing them together creating their incomparable magic on the screen. Further, looking at the last couple of decades, during which Ghai has repeatedly given many weak products in comparison to his cult films, it may end up as a dream that will remain unfulfilled.

Having said that, there is still a possibility that Ghai might release the valuable rushes of the shoot on his official online channel or website, remembering those days of glory. The writer-director had reportedly shot a song penned by Anand Bakshi and composed by Laxmikant Pyarelal, with Amitabh and others on screen in the first shooting schedule of a few days, which was loved by all. Hopefully, we will also get to hear the song and witness the footage, whenever the showman decides to reveal the treasure, taking it out of the archives of Mukta Arts.

CHAPTER THIRTY TWO

GULZAR AND HIS UNSEEN LIBAAS

The mid-'80s film *Libaas* holds special importance for every true fan of the legendary poet, lyricist, writer, and director Gulzar because of an interesting fact associated with its existence. The fact is that though the film was reportedly completed in 1986-88, it still has not been officially released either in the theaters, home video market, or any online portal.

So where at one end you can easily see its publicity posters and enjoy its worth listening soundtrack available on the Internet, the film remains to be seen by almost all Gulzar fans and is still untraceable even after four decades of its completion.

Based on the theme of extramarital affairs written around the background of a theater group, it features Naseeruddin Shah, Shabana Azmi, and Raj Babbar in key roles and has music by the maestro R. D. Burman with lyrics penned by Gulzar himself. Talking about a subject that was considered to be quite bold and path-breaking at that time, the film also had its struggle with the censor board and later could not be released due to some undisclosed issues related to its producer. However, it did win its due appreciation when screened at the International Film Festival of India four years later.

Apart from its unique extinct status, *Libaas* enjoys a mystical kind of aura around its existence mainly because of its four fabulous tracks which are, *Sili Hawa Chhoo Gayi, Khamosh Sa Afsana, Phir Kisi Shaakh Ne* and *Kya Bura Hai Kya Bhala* sung by Lata Mangeshkar, Suresh Wadekar and Burman himself. Its music cassettes were first released by *Weston* Audio company in the late '80s but later started coming on *Saregama* (then HMV) in combination with a few other Gulzar classics like *Ijaazat.*

Thankfully, the film is still available in two different forms except the usual moving images shot with the magical camera.

Adding to its unique features, *Libaas* was later written in the form of a short story by the writer-director himself with the title of *Chaabi (Key)*, which was published under the name of *Seema* in his compilation book *Raavi Paar. (So, it was the story based on the film and not the other way to be specific)*

Further elaborating on its short indicative storyline, the film's complete script has also been published in the form of a book by *Radhakrishan Publications,* Delhi. The book is also titled *Libaas* with a short introduction by Gulzar in which the veteran makes you aware of the unusual journey of his thoughtful creation from an unreleased film to a short story and then as a script in the form of a book based on the changing human relationships of our developing society.

As a pleasant surprise, *Libaas* was once again screened in the International Film Festival of India in 2014 (in Goa) after more than 25 years of its making to raise new hopes. At that event, it was indeed shocking to know from the director himself that even he had not seen the film post its completion back in the late '80s and had no information of its print in existence too.

In Gulzar's own words, he said, *"Yeh film aapne bhi nahin dekhi, maine bhi nahin dekhi. Aur main bhi aaj 25 saal ke baad issey dekh raha hun*".

The surprise continued in the year 2017 when it was reported that the film might be released soon in the theaters distributed by Zee Studios, and later it was stated that it might finally get released on the digital platform by the producers.

But unfortunately, we are still waiting for that to be true and hope it soon gets aired on any digital portal at least, reaching all the die-hard fans of the blessed maestro.

CHAPTER THIRTY THREE

ZAKHMI AURAT – THE BOLD FILM SUGGESTING CASTRATION FOR RAPISTS IN 1988

In the final decades of the last millennium, Hindi Cinema was more famous for its films full of action, songs, and romance, with its lead actors dancing around the trees representing a fantasy world. Though there was an important 'Thoughtful Art Cinema Wave' prevailing in the industry (beginning in the late '60s), still meaningful subjects were rarely adapted by the mainstream filmmakers in their films featuring popular stars. Multi-starrer action was the most followed genre in the '80s and these action dramas were being written on the sets as per the available dates and arrival of the featured stars.

In this creative chaos (as it should be called) there came an unusual action-revenge drama titled *Zakhmi Aurat (The Wounded Woman)* which deserves to be rated as an important trendsetter of that era led by a group of women. It delivered something shocking for the conservative mindset of the Indian viewers despite having all the usual songs, dance, and drama.

Made on the subject of increasing rapes in society (and we are talking about four decades back), the film suggested a dreadful punishment for the accused, wherein a gang of victimized women starts castrating all the rapists registered in the police records, who have escaped court cases with their influence and power of wealth.

No doubt the subject was bold enough for the Indian audience used to watching Doordarshan as the only TV channel in those years. But at the same time, the courageous project was also applauded a lot by the Indian women becoming the talk of the town for weeks through leading newspapers and magazines. Playing the second innings of her career, Dimple Kapadia enacted the lead role of a persecuted police officer going for her revenge. And the act is envied by many renowned Hindi film actresses to date as they rarely get to play such strong characters on screen in our male-oriented cinema.

Zakhmi Aurat had a relevant subject relating to India's present scenario, where brutal rapes and murders continue to be a disgusting menace to our society without any major change. The heinous instances of cruel rapes and murders of the victims are regularly there in the news reported in this third decade of the new millennium and our society and the political will is still confused and undecisive, even after the infamous Nirbhaya case involving inhuman torture.

The film did raise pertinent questions back in 1988 but the message never reached the people in power or the judiciary, continuing with the same old ineffective norms and laws resulting in painfully lengthy and insulting media and legal battles.

Now after almost four decades one wonders that had the lawmakers and judiciary worked upon suggestions like the one mentioned in the film back in the late '80s, then we would have certainly not reached the present pathetic situation, saving thousands of innocent girls and their suffering families.

But perhaps *Films* are just seen as *Films*, not considered capable of making any major constructive contribution to society, and we still haven't learned the fact that every artistic expression is nothing else but a mirror image of ourselves and our social structure.

Taking its major inspiration for the castration plot from the English film *The Ladies Club* (1986), with references from the controversial *I Spit On Your Grave* (1978), *Zakhmi Aurat* is admittedly just an average film as far as its direction and execution are concerned. But because this brave and unapologetic attempt was made way back in the late '80s, it does become an indisputable milestone of Hindi cinema making a courageous and unheard-of statement of its own. Moreover, it continues to remain a significant film after four decades of its release, as no one has dared to make another film/series on the subject, despite the OTT revolution giving all the liberties to the new-age writers and directors.

Unfortunately, one does not find *Zakhmi Aurat* quoted as a bold, prophetic film in widely promoted books and articles on Hindi Cinema. Its average making and box office performance is surely responsible for the omission. But that doesn't allow us to take away the credit from its team, thinking out of the box in the times when the entire industry was confused about what to make, bringing back the audience to the theatres.

Hence, the courage of director Avtar Bhogal and his team, along with Dimple Kapadia leading from the front, certainly deserve much more appreciation for such a rare, audacious venture predicting the needs of the future. Ironically, as depicted in the film, the situation hasn't gone through any major change and the women in our society are still waiting for a stern law against the crime, providing justice in time.

CHAPTER THIRTY FOUR

Three unusual & bold films from Hrishikesh Mukherjee based on sensitive themes

One of the most loved directors of the Hindi film industry, Hrishikesh Mukherjee is widely known for his light-hearted, comical dramas having many realistic and immensely likable characters adored by one and all. Holding a big repeat value, his films could easily make an instant connection with the viewers, especially those coming from a middle-class family, and are still fondly watched by the audiences after decades of their release. Known for their enjoyable content, perfect for the entire family together with many sweet life-teaching lessons for all age groups, Mukherjee's most popular works include *Anari, Aashirwad, Satyakam, Guddi, Anand, Bawarchi, Abhimaan, Mili, Namak Haraam, Chupke Chupke, Alaap, Golmaal, Khoobsoorat, Bemisal, Naram Garam* and more.

Out of his complete filmography, where only one film, *Buddha Mil Gaya,* revolves around a crime plot dealing with a few suspicious murders shown with a comic touch, we have three of his not-so-famous projects exploring some unusual and bold sexual themes, against the popular social image of the veteran director.

The first among the three is ***Sabse Bada Sukh*** (1972), comically pointing towards the biggest pleasure of life, i.e., 'sex' as dreamt by the young ones post the age of adolescence. Starring Vijay Arora, Robi Ghosh, Asrani, Utpal Dutt, Keshto Mukherjee, Rajnibala, and more, this is probably one of the first sex comedies made in Hindi cinema in the early '70s.

Its basic storyline is about the fantasies a small-town youngster (Vijay Arora) has about the beautiful film heroines of the Bombay film industry and how he reacts while witnessing the shooting of a film close to his village. In search of his *Sabse Bada Sukh*, he travels to Bombay with his supposedly clever friend who has already spent a few months in the city and the film portrays their weird experiences quite amusingly. With many straight satirical references to porn magazines, blue films, reputed Filmfare Awards, prostitution rackets, and much more, this is undoubtedly a surprising comedy coming from Hrishikesh Mukherjee, breaking many preset notions of Hindi cinema in the early '70s.

The second movie in this unusual genre is ***Jurmaana*** (1979), featuring Amitabh Bachchan, Vinod Mehra, Rakhee, Asrani, and A. K. Hangal in the lead roles, based on a story quite unlike a Hrishikesh Mukherjee subject to be released in that particular (conservative) era. Revolving around a bet between two school-time friends, the film has a rich Casanova-type grey character played by Amitabh, who confidently bets to bring the young introvert daughter of their old school teacher into his bedroom through his charm and money power.

Eventually, he manages to do the same under some different circumstances but the event completely changes the life of that poor innocent girl, feeling the shameful guilt forever.

Interestingly, the film could not win over the viewers due to its unusual theme but is still remembered for one of its fabulous tracks, *Saawan Ke Jhoole Padey* sung by Lata Mangeshkar, composed by R. D. Burman and penned by Anand Bakshi.

The third and almost unknown film in the category is ***Na-Mumkin*** (1988) which would be quite surprising for many since it talks about an old man marrying a young girl and then mysteriously committing suicide on his very first night of marriage. The shocking secret behind his sudden decision is that in search of a new companion in his old age, he unknowingly gets married to his young daughter by mistake. Hence, he commits suicide out of guilt realising the inhuman blunder made inadvertently.

Though the film later reveals the hidden reason behind their marriage, justifying the weird act, it should not be disclosed here to keep alive your interest and experience of watching *Na-Mumkin,* based on a strange subject or storyline, hugely different from the cinema Mukherjee is known for. Also, the film honestly is not a well-made one by the veteran, almost entirely shot abroad (facing various issues during its making) with a limited cast featuring Sanjeev Kumar, Dr. Shreeram Lagoo, and Om Shiv Puri (as the three old friends). It also had Zeenat Aman, Vinod Mehra and Raj Babbar representing the younger brigade.

So, in a career full of many memorable, must watch and exceptionally directed gems of Hindi cinema, these are three unusually bold and experimental films tried by Hrishikesh Mukherjee having a completely different genre and feel compared to his highly acclaimed repertoire of many famous films.

❖ ❖ ❖

Fact File: In addition to the surprising elements related to *Sabse Bada Sukh* – largely considered the first sex comedy of Hindi cinema – the film had its story and screenplay by Hrishikesh Mukherjee, additional scenes by Salil Chowdhary (also its music composer) and dialogues written by Gulzar (another unexpected name in the credits).

CHAPTER THIRTY FIVE

Subhash Ghai's KARZ and its two-way inspirational status

Subhash Ghai's *Karz* - a mixture of different genres (namely a musical, murder-mystery as well as a suspense and family drama) – was declared a semi-hit in certain regions and considered to be ahead of its times and unconventional by many trade analysts in 1980.

However, if we look back, then *Karz* enjoys a rare two-way inspirational status like very few films manage to do in our Hindi cinema. On one hand, it has a hugely inspired script as well as a few identical tracks borrowed from the West, but on the other, the film went on to inspire more than 10 Hindi and regional films in the country taking clear cues from its storyline, execution, and lyrics quite frequently.

Talking about the borrowed concepts first, though the film is said to be heavily inspired by the English flick *The Reincarnation of Peter Proud* released in 1975, the other known fact remains that Hindi cinema had already made a highly successful film on the subject of reincarnation as *Madhumati* way back in 1958. So, the subject was quite clearly not being introduced 'for the first time ever' as projected. Next, apart from the basic plot, its melodious soundtrack composed by *Laxmikant Pyarelal* also had some uncanny resemblances with the creations of Western artists like George Benson and Lord Shorty, which surely pointed towards inspirational liberty taken for some unknown reasons.

Coming to the films inspired by Subhash Ghai's *Karz,* it was officially remade as *Enakkul Oruvan* (1984) in Tamil, *Aatma Balam* (1985) in Telugu, and *Yuga Purusha* (1989) in Kannada, with most recent adaptation being the Hindi film *Karzzzz* (2008) starring Himesh Reshammiya and Urmila in the lead. But before Himesh, Farah Khan also came up with her re-worked version of the same theme in *Om Shanti Om* (2007) and for that, she even planned a respectable tribute by beginning the film with a restored song footage of the original *Karz* featuring both Rishi Kapoor and Subhash Ghai dancing on the screen (made possible through the digital revolution and computer graphics). Plus, she also got a new track specially arranged by Pyarelal to honour his majestic contribution to Hindi cinema – an appreciable nice gesture from the choreographer-turned-director indeed.

Later, the film's name and a few key phrases of its various songs inspired seven films in all, including *Karz - The Burden of Truth* (2002), reusing the same title with a new tag line and *Dard-e-Dil* (1983), *Paisa Yeh Paisa* (1985), *Main Solha Baras Ki* (1998), *Ek Hasina Thi* (2004), *Aashiq Banaya Aapne* (2005) and *Om Shanti Om* (2007) – borrowing their titles from the lyrics or various mukhdas of the songs in *Karz's* hit soundtrack.

Other than this rare two-way inspirational status, *Karz* also had some unique special points in its execution too as mentioned below:

1. It was a project based on the upbeat, trendy Disco music, which was the forte of the legendary R. D. Burman in that era. So many were shockingly surprised when Ghai chose Laxmikant Pyarelal as his music directors, more known as the masters of Indian musical arrangements and instruments. However, what Laxmikant Pyarelal did for *Karz* proved Subhash Ghai right without any doubt.
2. Similar to his odd choice for the music directors, another unusual casting opted by Ghai was roping in Simi Garewal for a major role, and that too of a killer woman or a vamp, something she had never played before.
3. Despite being given a powerful persona as the villain, Prem Nath did not have a single dialogue in the film and he only conveyed through a tapping sound made on various things like glass, phone receiver, etc.
4. With *Karz*, Subhash Ghai also introduced a useful concept of brand promotion on the screen and promoted the music company *HMV* boldly with some innovative stage designs. For instance, just watch the whole dance sequence of Rishi Kapoor in his opening song where he is dancing on a giant record and the music company's name is written in big letters all over in the background.
5. The soundtrack had all songs sung by Kishore Kumar as he was a perfect choice for the genre suiting Rishi Kapoor playing the lead. But Laxmikant-Pyarelal were too keen to use the voice of Mohd. Rafi for one soulful ghazal *Dard-e-Dil* in the film picturized on Kapoor. Later, both Kishore Kumar's *Om Shanti Om* and Mohd. Rafi's *Dard-e-Dil* got nominated in the Best Male Singer and Best Lyrics category for the 1981 Filmfare Awards. Interestingly, Kishore Kumar won the award

for *Hazaar Rahein* from *Thodi Si Bewafai* that year defeating *Karz's* innovative creations.

Hence, though *Karz* managed to achieve only moderate success at the box office in its initial year of release, the film deserves to be rated as a cult, path-breaking entertainer of the '80s and unarguably a must-watch musical for all young lovers of Hindi cinema and its music.

CHAPTER THIRTY SIX

Music Director Ravi's unforgettable relationship with our personal lives

One of the most talented but underrated music directors of the Indian film industry was Ravi Shankar Sharma, popularly known as Ravi, who left this world for his next musical journey on 7th March 2012. But this is not an 'Obituary' for the genius as I simply don't believe or like writing such pieces just after the death of any great personality. Reading all those posthumous articles published everywhere makes you feel as if we get the time to remember such great men simply after their deaths and not before that.

So, this is about a rare and interesting fact I wish to share about Ravi's incomparable creations for many successful Hindi films and their seldom-mentioned relationship with our personal lives.

Not many know that Ravi began as a chorus singer with famous music directors of his times before assisting Hemant Kumar and later contributing as an independent music director. But what differentiates his work from others is the fact that even after more than half a century, his compositions have an immortal, unique, and amazing relationship with the personal life of every Hindi film music lover, which is rarely discussed or mentioned by historians and enthusiasts of Hindi cinema. In fact, the deep connection of our personal memories with his few exclusive creations cannot be denied or overlooked by any means.

To be specific, the tracks mentioned below highlight Ravi as the only music director who became an integral part of the personal lives of his listeners like nobody else, irrespective of whether the person was his huge fan or not.

Coming to the point, Hindi film music remains hugely incomplete if we take out the following three cult songs from its colossal repertoire. Over the last seven decades, these tracks have been a part of the essential social events in the marriage functions of every Bollywood fan expressing various emotions.

1. ***Aaj Mere Yaar Ki Shaadi Hai*** (*Aadmi Sadak Ka* (1977)/ Mohd. Rafi/Verma Malik) The song was and is still played by brass band groups in *Baraat processions* as the key feature of a marriage, making all friends dance together.
2. ***Babul Ki Duayen Leti Ja*** (*Neel Kamal* (1968)/Mohd. Rafi/Sahir Ludhianvi) This is again a song religiously played at the time of *Doli* or *Bidaai* of the girl from her parents' home after the marriage ceremony. Further, it is also essentially inserted in the video coverage of marriages to date.
3. ***Aye Meri Zohrazabin, Tujhe Maloom Nahin*** (*Waqt* (1965)/Manna Dey/Sahir Ludhianvi) A song that is played or sung at every *Sangeet* ceremony (a musical get-together on the eve of a marriage) involving all the lovable elders of the family creating an atmosphere of fun

and celebration. Plus, any DJ cannot just survive without having this particular track in his collection while going to perform at an Indian wedding anywhere in the world.

The fact that all these songs have been composed by only one person, Ravi, clearly proves that his music was and will always remain associated with the personal lives of all Hindi film music lovers, without any doubt.

In addition, there are five more songs, which nine out of ten times come to our mind whenever we try to express the following human emotions through a film song.

1. ***Chanda Mama Door Ke*** from Ravi's debut film *Vachan* (1955) as a composer as well as lyricist (also the debut film of Rajendra Kumar/sung by Asha Bhosle) - This is one of the most famous *lullabies (cradle song)* in the country and popular as a cult children poem since decades. Interestingly, many don't even relate it to the movie considering it a traditional kids' rhyme taught in the pre-primary schools even today.
2. ***Dadi Amma Dadi Amma Maan Jao*** (*Gharana* (1961)/ Asha Bhosle-Kamal Barot/Shakeel Badauni) The second most famous children's song that is again widely sung by kids in their homes as well as at schools as a lovable granny song. It is probably the first song one would recall representing the adorable relationship between the kids and their grandmothers.
3. ***Chaudhvin Ka Chand Ho*** (*Chaudhvin Ka Chand* (1961)/ Mohd. Rafi/Shakeel Badauni) The song instantly strikes us the moment we wish to praise a beautiful woman. Husbands often sing this to impress their wives as they are dressing up for any special occasion and lovers use the expression more than often.
4. ***Dil Ke Armaan Aansuon Mein Beh Gaye*** (*Nikaah* (1982)/Salma Agha/Hassan Kamaal) This phrase at

once comes to our mind whenever we have to express grief, sorrow, or sadness through a song. The line is also many times used in a comical manner, to add some fun quotient to otherwise tense moments of life.

5. ***Garibon Ki Suno, Woh Tumhari Sunega*** (*Dus Lakh* (1966)/Mohd. Rafi-Asha Bhosle/Ravi) The opening lines of this song were commonly used by beggars asking for food or money at roadside or traffic signals in India. The song is still used in sequences focusing on begging or beggars in both stage plays and films.

Again, these five songs have been composed by only one person, Ravi, with the last one even sharing a spiritual thought pointing towards the theory of *Karma,* penned by the veteran himself.

The genius not only composed for over 70 Hindi films (including many Jubilee hits) but also sang a few songs during the initial days of his career and composed music for more than 15 Malayalam films, with the majority becoming regional hits. The success eventually earned him a new name *Bombay Ravi,* fondly given by the industry people in the south. This is yet another amazing and lesser-known fact associated with the master music director, whose creations will continue to be part of every Indian family function forever.

CHAPTER THIRTY SEVEN

UTPAL DUTT – NOT JUST A COMEDIAN

Utpal Dutt, who is largely remembered for his famous comical acts in cult comedies such as *Gol Maal, Lakhon Ki Baat, Rang Birangi, Shaukeen*, and more by the Hindi film viewers, was a multifaceted creative personality with some lesser discussed but astonishing capabilities, more known to the Bengali films and their theatre audiences.

Putting it honestly, it's a pity that the Hindi audiences mostly know this great thinker as a mere comedian saying *"achhaaaaa"* & *"eeee....shhh"* in his impeccable style in all those entertaining comedies, and only a few know about his great insightful works with a background of an eminent theatre activist, filmmaker & writer in Bengal.

During the creative phase of his life between 1929 and 1993, Dutt was not only a remarkable actor but also an inspirational writer-playwright and a director too, beginning his *'Little Theatre Group'* as a contributing step towards the growth of modern Indian theatre in the late '40s. Later, his writings and plays started depicting the political state of the world/country full of revolutionary ideas challenging the system itself, for which he even had to go underground and was also jailed in those years of evolution of Indian theatre in the last century.

Dutt acted in about 200 Bengali and Hindi films in his illustrious career and gave many splendid noteworthy performances in classics like Mrinal Sen's *Bhuvan Shome* (1969-National Award for Best Actor), Satyajit Ray's *Agantuk* along with *Gol Maal, Naram Garam, Rang Birangi* & *Saheb* – winning Filmfare Awards for Best Comic Actor & Supporting Roles proving his versatile talent. The *Sangeet Natak Akademi* awarded him the reputed *Fellowship for Lifetime Contribution to Theatre* in the year 1990. Plus, apart from the plays, Dutt also directed more than six Bengali films and one Hindi project in the mid-'80s.

As a prolific writer, he penned numerous articles, reviews & seminar papers in his career spanning around four decades. At present (apart from the ones in Bengali) his five books compiled in English are available for all interested friends, published by Seagull Books of Kolkata, namely *Towards a Revolutionary Theatre, Three Plays: Hunting the Sun-The Great Rebellion-Nightmare City, Rights of Man, On Theatre* and *On Cinema.*

His bold and inspiring writings tell you a lot about the astonishing knowledge, keen eye, and impressive analytical vision this creative man possessed in his powerful identity. His books introduce the reader to a completely different Utpal Dutt who had an amazing understanding of all kinds of cinema and its maestros known in other parts of the world too. He was a person who had a lot to talk about the personal, social, and moral responsibilities of a creative artist, other than just enjoying the riches coming along with the success achieved in his respective field. Sadly, Dutt is not widely known for his more important qualities to the majority of Indian film lovers in the Hindi belt.

At times, such is the passionate honesty in his chosen words that it surprises you about how rebellious he used to be in his seminars and public meetings without any fear of a controversy creating differences with his fellow filmmakers or any government action taken against him for expressing provocative thoughts.

This was the original Utpal Dutt, the true artist, and I bet almost 90 percent of the Hindi movie-watching population would be unaware of this hidden powerful persona of the thinking actor-writer-director, who flawlessly played *Bhawani Shanker*, the moustache-loving employer of Amol Palekar in *Gol Maal.*

However, I am sure after reading this article, no one (among the Hindi film viewers) in the future will ever treat the veteran creative genius as only a comedian.

CHAPTER THIRTY EIGHT

GUIDE - A SECRET IN ITS SOUNDTRACK

Guide (1966), a masterpiece with eternal music remains one of the best creations of the Hindi film industry that is acclaimed the world over. The music director of this epic film, S. D. Burman, was a Navketan's (Dev Anand's production company) loyalist and Dev had full confidence in him and his ability to create magical notes for his onscreen characters as required.

For their film *Guide*, Dev and Vijay Anand wanted only S. D. Burman as the music director and they finally got him on board after a long wait since Burman was recovering from an illness. Reciprocating the trust shown, Burman came up with a memorable score for the film contributing a lot to the mesmerising impact of *Guide* on its viewers worldwide. But there is one amazing secret in the brilliantly composed soundtrack of the film not known to many.

The musical secret is related to the film's two immensely popular songs penned by Shailendra and sung by Lata Mangeshkar and Mohd. Rafi in their solo renditions.

1. *Mosey Chhal Kiye Jaaye* by Lata Mangeshkar and
2. *Kya Se Kya Ho Gaya* by Mohd. Rafi

Here the unbelievable and surprising twist is that the genius composer not only used the same *raga* for these two songs but actually used the same notes or a similar tune for both tracks in such a manner (with a difference of half a note) that they never turn out to be identical to anyone listening until the fact is revealed to them specifically.

In fact, even in the film, the songs are played back-to-back as two similar expressions of betrayal coming from the female and male perspectives one after the other. Yet it does not strike the viewers and they do not realise that the two songs in reality have similar compositions presented in different scales, different moods, and with contrasting musical arrangements. Besides, *Mosey Chhal Kiye Jaaye* is also the only song in which the renowned santoor maestro Pandit Shiv Kumar Sharma played the tabla as a friendly gesture for the Burmans.

So, if you re-visit the classic, just listen to the two unforgettable gems once again and this time try to find the hidden secret in their compositions as revealed above.

❖ ❖ ❖

Fact File: The film's soundtrack also remains one of the rarest, featuring two songs sung by the maestro S. D. Burman - '*Wahan Kaun Hai Tera*' and '*Allah Megh De.*'

Section Two

CHAPTER THIRTY NINE

WHEN TWO UNHEARD ANTRAS OF *EK PYAR KA NAGHMA HAI* FROM SHOR WERE LATER USED IN TWO DIFFERENT FILMS

The immortal song *Ek Pyar Ka Naghma Hai* from *Shor* (1972) is rated among the most beautiful creations of that era, explaining life and its meaningful twists with very simple yet expressive words, well-chosen by one of Hindi cinema's most talented but forgotten and underrated lyricists/poets, Santosh Anand.

Melodiously composed by Laxmikant Pyarelal and soulfully sung by Lata Mangeshkar and Mukesh, such is the magic in this spirited song that it infuses positive energy into the listener like a life-saving drug given just at the right time. Thus, the song deservingly finds its place in the most memorable hits of the last century, especially from the golden era of Hindi cinema before the '80s.

Here, a fascinating and hidden fact about its lyrics is that Santosh had written two more antras that were not recorded as part of the song included in the film Shor. The unused antras were later used in two different films in 1974 and 1992. But before revealing the names of those movies, first, let us cherish those two unheard verses as below:

"Jo Beet Gaya Hai Woh, Ab Daur Na Aayega,
Is Dil Mein Siva Tere, Koi Aur Na Aayega,
Ghar Phoonk Diya Humne, Ab Raakh Uthaani Hai,
Zindagi Aur Kuchh Bhi Nahin, Teri Meri Kahaani Hai!

Tum Saath Na Do Mera, Chalna Mujhe Aata Hai,
Har Aag Se Waaqif Hun, Jalna Mujhe Aata Hai,
Tadbeer Ke Hathon Se, Taqdeer Banani Hai,
Zindagi Aur Kuchh Bhi Nahin, Teri Meri Kahaani Hai!"

Manoj Kumar used the opening couplet of the second verse "*Tum Saath Na Do Mera.....*" by changing it to "*Koi Saath Na De Mera........*" as one of his own dialogues in the 1974 film *Roti Kapda Aur Makaan* in the sequence when Shashi Kapoor and Zeenat Aman meet him in a party.

Later, 20 years after the original creation, the lyricist incorporated the opening lines from both these unused *antras* in his song *Dil Deewane Ka Dola Dildaar Ke Liye* in its sad part filmed on Dharmendra for the film *Tahalka* released in 1992.

And in the present, with all my love and respect towards the original creators, here are five extended antras/verses of the song that I wrote as my vision towards life inspired by the spirit of the soulful track in the first decade of the new millennium.

Tum Saath Agar Hotey, Aasaa(n) Yeh Dagar Hoti,
Main Chain Se Jee Leta, Tum Paas Agar Hoti,
Kuchh Beet Gayi Apni, Kuchh Aur Bitaani Hai,
Zindagi Aur Kuchh Bhi Nahin, Teri Meri Kahaani Hai!

Dukh Hai To Sukh Bhi Hai, Dono Ka Bichhona Hai,
Ik Khel Hai Yeh Jeevan, Hota Hai Jo Hona Hai,
Umrhey Hue Baadal Ne, Bijlee Bhi Giraani Hai,
Zindagi Aur Kuchh Bhi Nahin, Teri Meri Kahaani Hai!

Gar Dhoop Hai Yeh Jeevan, Yahaan Shaam Bhi Aati Hai,
Har Gham Ki Ghata Do Din, Aakar Chali Jaati Hai,
Aansoo Na Baha Aye Dil, Yeh Reet Purani Hai,
Zindagi Aur Kuchh Bhi Nahin, Teri Meri Kahaani Hai!

Woh Dekh Raha Hai Sab, Tu Uska Khilona Hai,
Yeh Daur Hain Jeevan Ke, Aisa Bhi Kya Rona Hai,
Usi Ek Sahaare Ne, Bigrhi Bhi Banani Hai,
Zindagi Aur Kuchh Bhi Nahin, Teri Meri Kahaani Hai!

Kuch Aur Thehar Aye Dil, Jeena Tujhe Aayega,
Ik Khaas Ada Tujhko, Dushman Bhi Sikhayega,
Baazi Jo Laagayi Hai, Woh Jeet Ke Jaani Hai,
Zindagi Aur Kuchh Bhi Nahin, Teri Meri Kahaani Hai!

Ek Pyar Ka Naghma Hai, Maujon Ki Rawaani Hai,
Zindagi Aur Kuchh Bhi Nahin, Teri Meri Kahaani Hai!

Hope you find these new antras/verses useful and worth remembering along with the cult song.

Cheers to the Masters!

CHAPTER FORTY

Amitabh Bachchan-Bally Sagoo's Music Album ABY BABY and its link with the icon's 3 films

In the mid-'90s, the music scene in India was dominated by Pop music and videos, with repeated telecasts on both MTV and VTV (the two close competitors) influencing young music lovers. One of the most popular artists of that era was Bally Sagoo, who had made a grand entry into the world of both Pop and remix versions of songs such as *Jhoole Jhoole Laal* by Ustad Nusrat Fateh Ali Khan, *Gurh Nalon Ishq Mitha* by Malkit Singh and the immensely famous re-sung version of *Chura Liya Hai Tumne Jo Dil Ko* from the film *Yaadon Ki Baraat* (1973). Widely credited as the pioneer of the remix revolution in the '90s, Bally operated from the U.K. as an artist of Oriental Star Agencies (Birmingham).

In the same part of the decade, Amitabh Bachchan also launched his audio company BIG B owned by the *Amitabh Bachchan Corporation Limited*, and released an outstanding soundtrack of Shekhar Kapur's controversial film *Bandit Queen* that had music by Ustad Nusrat Fateh Ali Khan making his debut in an Indian Hindi film as a music director and singer.

Interestingly, both Amitabh Bachchan and Bally Sagoo joined hands to bring out a private music album for BIG B music label that soon became the most awaited project after its official announcement. The album recorded in Bally's studio in England was finally released in 1996 titled ABY BABY (with BPL as sponsors printed on the sleeve). It created a buzz getting some good initial sales due to an entertaining comical video, *Eer Beer Phattey,* featuring three school-going kids and a comic Amitabh Bachchan as a villager.

The second video was the remix of the famous title track from the film *Kabhi Kabhie* sung by Sadhna Sargam featuring the poetic dialogues in the icon's baritone voice. It portrayed Amitabh as a sculptor with Shobhana as his model or muse (a National Award-winning actress as well as a trained Bharata Natyam dancer), and the album had a saxophone instrumental version of the song too as its closing track.

The two video songs worked well in the beginning but the rest couldn't win over the listeners despite having rich literary value. While two of those tracks were unexciting remixes of Amitabh's *Mere Angne Mein* from the film *Laawaris* and *Khaike Paan Banaras Wala* from *Don*, the remaining two were folk-based songs penned by renowned Indian poet and Bachchan's father, Late Sh. Harivansh Rai Bachchan. The tracks had catchy compositions and lyrics as *Javo Lavo Piya Nadiya Se Son Machari* and *Aaj Mehenga Hai Saiyaan Rupaiya Re* giving the listener a completely different flavour and feel. But they somehow didn't work and probably would have sounded much better with a more Indian rhythm as used in the main *Eer Beer Phattey* track.

Unfortunately, the album remains unavailable in the market today since the company is not operational anymore. But you can still hear its tracks and watch the videos posted by fans at online portals, like YouTube, remembering the musical era. ABY BABY remains the favourite of many like-minded friends interested in such experimental projects and I later came to know that its creative music videos were directed by none other than the veteran director Rakeysh Omprakash Mehra in his initial years.

Coming to the second part of the chapter, there happens to be a link between Amitabh's *Aby Baby* and one of his '70s hit movies titled *Adalat*. The fun-filled song *Eer Bir Phattey* also features in the 1976 film, in which Amitabh plays a simple, innocent villager fooled by cunning industrialists.

Being one of those numerous films getting their basic inspiration from the western classic *The Godfather* (as clearly indicated in one of its original posters too), *Adalat* had Amitabh Bachchan in a double role of a father and son with conflicting interests. At the beginning of the film, three industrialists visit the village looking for a tiger hunt and they ask Amitabh to help them out in their leisure sport, to which he readily agrees. While guiding his three guests in the jungle, he keeps singing the opening lines of the song *Eer Bir Phattey* as *Eer Kahen Chalo Sher Maar Aayi, Beer Kahen Chalo Sher Maar Aayi* in his comic style. The same song was later adapted as a stand-alone track in his Pop album *Aby Baby.*

Playing a similar kind of role of a simpleton villager in his 1981 hit *Yaarana,* Amitabh sang another song from the album *Javo Lavo Piya Nadiya Se Son Machhri* while making food for his friend Amjad Khan at the beginning of the film before becoming a singing star.

In addition, Amitabh can also be seen casually singing *Mehenga Hai Saiyan Rupaiya* from the same album in one of the scenes of his film *Pyar Ki Kahani* (1971) showcasing his keen personal liking to the songs.

So next time you catch *Adalat, Yaraana,* or *Pyar Ki Kahani* online or on a TV channel, then just watch out for these sequences featuring the songs and enjoy.

CHAPTER FORTY ONE

THE SPIRITUAL FACTOR CONNECTING SILSILA (1981) AND RAB NE BANA DI JODI (2008)

The topic might seem to be a little confusing, but there does indeed exist a hidden devotional factor common in both *Silsila* and *Rab Ne Bana Di Jodi* from Yash Raj Films, featuring the legendary stars of the Hindi film industry.

The spiritual element connecting the two is a *Sikh* devotional hymn or *Shabad* that was a part of both the soundtracks, sung in the same composition, by the same performer, in exactly the same style, but in two different eras mentioned below.

In 1981, Yash Chopra used the *Shabad* with the divine words *Baanh Jinah Di Pakadiye* (*meaning*: when we hold our beloved Guru's hand) in the soundtrack of *Silsila* (included in the initially released set of two LPs), rendered by Bhai Harbans Singh Jagadhari Wale, in a soothing composition as per its enlightening words.

Then after 27 years, in 2008, Aditya Chopra, under the expert guidance of his father Yash Chopra, again used the same *Shabad* in his prestigious project *Rab Ne Bana Di Jodi* featuring Shah Rukh

Khan and the debutant Anushka Sharma in the lead, with a story revolving around a Punjabi backdrop. This time, the *Shabad* was used as the background track for the opening sequence of the film when the viewers are introduced to the divine city of Amritsar on the screen, amidst a Punjabi ambience.

And once again the *Shabad* was re-recorded in the voice of Bhai Harbans Singh Jagadhari Wale only, sung in the same old composition as earlier there in the original soundtrack of *Silsila* (but with a change of note/scale).

That is how YRF's *Silsila* (1981) and *Rab Ne Bana Do Jodi* (2008) are spiritually connected to each other through a devotional track.

CHAPTER FORTY TWO

WHAT'S COMMON BETWEEN PAA & BAWARCHI?

Paa, released in 2009, was widely acclaimed both by the masses and the classes as it had many 'firsts' related to the amazing acting skills of the entire cast and the technical brilliance achieved by the crew. But here, instead of talking about the film's much-discussed status as a cinematic masterpiece with splendid performances, the extremely painstaking makeup of Big B, and his effortless portrayal of a child's character suffering from Progeria, I would like to mention another innovation tried by director R. Balki in the film's opening titles, wherein Jaya Bachchan appears on the screen and reads out all the credits with her calm, divine, motherly smile, and an effortless ease.

The director reportedly said in an interview that he thought of this idea as he was really very keen on working with Jaya and this gave him an opportunity without waiting for any other project to start. But for the record, the idea was not a 'first' as it had been earlier adapted by veteran director Hrishikesh Mukherjee in his famous movie *Bawarchi* made in 1972, which had Rajesh Khanna in the lead and Jaya playing the role of a daughter of the house, loved by one and all.

As seen in *Paa*, Mukherjee's *Bawarchi* also opens with a curtain on the screen and a voice-over of Amitabh, who reads out all the respective credits in a mix of Hindi and English. But here, the major difference is that the credits do not appear on the screen and the viewers only hear the voice, like that of a *Sutradhar*.

However, the most interesting (rather balancing) part of this comparison is that while in 1972, *Bawarchi* was the movie in which Jaya played a prominent role and Amitabh (who did not feature in it) gave his voice-over for the credits, in 2009, *Paa* was the movie where Amitabh played a prominent role and Jaya (who did not feature in it) gave her voice-over for its credits along with her warm and gracious presence.

I strongly believe that with this inspired insertion in their home production *Paa*, both Amitabh and Jaya actually gave a humble tribute to their favourite and one of the most respected directors of the Hindi film industry, Hrishikesh Mukherjee.

❖ ❖ ❖

Fact File: With *Paa,* the father-son duo (Amitabh-Abhishek) also made a rare record of its kind playing reverse roles on screen, where the son played the father and the father played the son like never before in the history of Indian cinema.

CHAPTER FORTY THREE

THE LINK BETWEEN NASEEB, DHARAM VEER, OM SHANTI OM AND KALA BAZAR

Acclaimed director Manmohan Desai truly knew the art of how to convincingly entertain his audience with a pleasant mix of emotion, drama, action, and comedy. His most successful films always had a charming 'feel good' factor and he often added a lovable surprise in his ventures to entertain the common man.

One of those great but hard-to-execute surprises was there in his film *Naseeb* released in 1981, wherein he filmed a party sequence and got together many reputed names of those times (mostly from Desai's earlier films) dancing on one platform as never before like a big loving family. The party was filmed on the song *John Johny Janardan* which had Amitabh Bachchan playing the entertaining singer cum waiter serving famous actors, including Raj Kapoor, Shammi Kapoor, Dharmendra, Waheeda Rehman, Mala Sinha, Indrani Mukherjee, Simi Grewal, Rajesh Khanna, Sharmila Tagore, Prem Chopra, Shakti Kapoor, Randhir

Kapoor, Rakesh Roshan, Bindu, Simple Kapadia, Prema Narayan and Vijay Arora.

In fact, the song shot by Jal Mistry and choreographed by Kamal also had Raj Kapoor – with whom Desai began his career in *Chhalia* – sportingly playing the accordion in his famous style. Just imagine what gala time they all must have had in those few days of shooting this particular song when there were no personal vanity vans and everyone had to sit together before the next shot.

Now the interesting link here is that the party that is being celebrated within the song is staged as the Golden Jubilee (50 weeks) celebration of the film *Dharam Veer* which was also the directorial venture of Manmohan Desai, released four years back in early 1977. And in the song, you can clearly see the backdrop saying *Dharam Veer* Golden Jubilee along with the standing cut-outs of both Dharmendra and Jeetendra on either side of the main gate.

Cut to the present era, taking a clear inspiration from this party scene, director-choreographer Farah Khan inserted a similar sequence in her 2007 film *Om Shanti Om* after more than 25 years of *Naseeb*. It had Shah Rukh Khan (playing the role of a successful actor) celebrating his film party in the title song *Deewangi Deewangi* with all present film celebrities entering the premises exactly in the same style as seen in the song *John Johny Janardan* with a particular signature tune being played in the background.

However, one major technical difference between the two songs is that in *Naseeb* all the veterans are standing together in the same frame and dancing with each other (i.e. shooting together). Whereas in *Om Shanti Om*, we have mostly individual entries (or in pairs), intelligently edited into a complete final version wherein it seems they are all together but in reality they are not and have given the partial shots alone as per their available time. Probably that is how both the era and times have changed, evident in this thoughtful comparison.

Interestingly, the only common person in both songs is *He-Man* Dharmendra, dancing along with his son Bobby Deol in the *Om Shanti Om* track. But more importantly in this new-age version, Jeetendra, who was the missing main lead in that Golden Jubilee party of *Dharam Veer,* makes his presence felt alongside his son Tushar Kapoor. Another star-son seen here is Saif Ali Khan, who had his mother featured in the *Naseeb* star-studded sequence along with Rajesh Khanna.

Concluding the comparison, the two sequences mentioned above can rightly be considered an indicative screen account of the change of generations in the last few decades, both conceived and executed superbly by their respective directors.

Having said that, the fact remains that before Manmohan Desai, director Vijay Anand mooted this idea with a slight change from his film *Kala Bazaar* released in 1960. To innovate, Anand used the real-life footage of prominent film celebrities attending the premiere of Mehboob Khan's *Mother India* in his film, making it a part of the script. Dev Anand and his friends were shown as black marketeers selling tickets at the event, while fans could be seen greeting the stars as they walked in smiling and waving at them.

❖ ❖ ❖

Fact File – Adding to its unique features, the LP record of *Naseeb* Soundtrack was released in a round sleeve instead of the usual square one, and it was printed in silver as a replica of a one-rupee coin with '*Naseeb*' – 1981 inscribed on it.

Section Three

CHAPTER FORTY FOUR

Na Kajre Ki Dhaar From MOHRA – Originally sung By Mukesh and the hidden, unexplored gems of the masters

Multi-starrer revenge thriller *Mohra* released in 1994 got hugely famous mainly due to a controversy surrounding its hit but highly inspired song *Tu Cheez Badi Hai Mast Mast.* The track followed exactly similar notes used in Ustad Nusrat Fateh Ali Khan's devotional track *Dum Mast Qalander Mast Mast* included in his album *Magic Touch.*

However, along with this immensely popular number, there was another song in its soundtrack that was universally accepted and loved by music lovers all over because of its melodious composition and beautiful lyrics. It was *Na Kajre Ki Dhaar, Na Motiyon Ke Haar, Na Koi Kiya Shringaar, Phir Bhi Kitni Sundar Ho.*

Honestly, when I first heard this fabulous track, I was really confused as somehow it seemed to be a misfit in a soundtrack composed by the tech-savvy *Viju Shah* (son of Kalyanji of the

Kalyanji-Anandji duo). The song had the same feel and tone as heard in all the great unforgettable gems from the golden era of Hindi film music. Moreover, though it did have some high notes, still the composition strongly compelled the listener to think of only one singer, *Mukesh,* as the track had his voice written all over it.

Accepting the fact, it was certainly sung well in the film by the famous ghazal singer Pankaj Udhas. But I always had some kind of doubt at the back of my mind whenever I used to play the song, till I heard a different version as a pleasant surprise that eventually confirmed all my doubts about its rendition expressed above.

The newly found track was remarkably sung by the one and only Mukesh in an old recording with the same lyrics originally written by Indivar.

No doubt, the song in reality was composed and recorded by Kalyanji-Anandji for a film that unfortunately got shelved and couldn't be completed. Later, when Viju Shah started his career as a music director, he intelligently used the same composition and lyrics in *Mohra*, also including the identical musical pieces (interludes) recorded by the legendary duo. He then brought in Pankaj Udhas to sing it in his soft velvet voice as required and the song finally got revived reaching its audience.

So, while my doubt was confirmed, it also made me think that there certainly ought to be many other precious undiscovered gems still lying somewhere in the forgotten or ignored archives of all the master composers from the golden era. Unfortunately, most of them would probably get lost and never reach their listeners due to the same old conflict between art and real-life complexities.

Thankfully, Yash Chopra began a valuable tradition by setting an example of reviving such hidden unheard compositions by the maestros in his film *Veer-Zaara* (2004), incorporating the well-preserved, unused works of Late Madan Mohan. But sadly, nobody seems to be interested in continuing it further. As a result, we are fast moving away from the rich legacy of unforgettable and melodious Hindi film songs that once happened to be the forte of our Indian cinema.

❖ ❖ ❖

Fact File: The key track of *Veer-Zaara* was originally a composition made for the song *"Dil Dhoondhta Hai"* in Gulzar's *Mausam (1976)* by the maestro Madan Mohan. It later got used as *"Tere Liye"* by Yash Chopra after more than three decades, successfully winning the hearts of the new generation.

CHAPTER FORTY FIVE

IMTIAZ ALI IN ANURAG KASHYAP'S BLACK FRIDAY AND MORE ABOUT THE CULT, TRENDSETTING FILM

It is not widely known that Imtiaz Ali, the famous director acclaimed for his intense love stories *Jab We Met, Love Aaj Kal, Rockstar, Highway* and *Tamasha,* started with directing TV serials and then also had a short acting stint early in his career under the direction of Anurag Kashyap.

It was the time when Hindi cinema had just started knocking at the door of a new-age thought process and many fresh innovative minds/directors were trying to break free from the (typical) default mode of the Hindi film industry with their bold attempts. Anurag Kashyap was one of those few thinking directors at that time working on his authentic docu-drama titled *Black Friday (2004),* after moving on from his unreleased debut movie *Paanch.* It revealed the story behind the 1993 bomb blasts that entirely changed the way Bombay (now Mumbai) used to be. Unfortunately, *Black Friday* also got stuck in the censors for a long time before it could reach its target audiences in 2007.

Apart from having established names like Pawan Malhotra, the film had numerous under-rated actors from the Hindi film industry, including Kay Kay Menon, Nawazuddin Siddiqui, Zakir Hussain, Pankaj Jha, Aditya Srivastava, Kishore Kadam, Pratima Kazmi and more, who later earned recognition in many major films.

Incidentally, this was also the only movie in which director Imtiaz Ali played a small yet important character, who enters into the narration towards its climax. If you have seen *Black Friday,* then you must have recognised Imtiaz minus his curly hair. But if you somehow missed spotting the director, then do watch it again as he was the one who played the character of *Yakub Memon,* the brother of mastermind *Tiger Memon,* in the movie.

An upsetting but realistic recreation of events before and after the blasts, the brilliantly scripted film was based on S. Hussain Zaidi's book *'Black Friday - The True Story of the Bombay Bomb Blasts'.* But as revealed by Kashyap in his interview, the most talked about lengthy chase sequence in it was neither part of the script nor the book, added as an afterthought. Interestingly, the same sequence also incorporates a dialogue from *Amar Akbar Anthony* inserted just at the right moment enhancing its powerful impact on the viewers.

Shot in an unusually realistic manner on actual locations, *Black Friday* had its background score and soundtrack composed by the famous band Indian Ocean (as their debut film project) with lyrics by Piyush Mishra. It included a thoughtful song *Arey Ruk Ja Re Bandey* which contributed a lot in conveying a relevant social message to the audience.

Not allowed to be released by the censor board in India, the film got leaked through pirated DVDs and kept winning appreciation and awards at Film Festivals abroad, resulting in a strange scenario. Further, as per Kashyap, the film got a new lease of life when a judge of the Supreme Court of India watched it in Dubai and considered the director's balanced approach worth reaching the audience. Surprisingly, *Black Friday* didn't prove to be a major success at the box office when it finally got released, because most of the people interested had already seen it.

However, as usual, the film deservingly got its cult status of a trendsetter when it was praised and acknowledged by a director from the West, Danny Boyle, who reportedly based the opening chase sequence of his Oscar-winning *Slumdog Millionaire* on the much-appreciated chase scene in *Black Friday.*

Perhaps we still have not learned to discover and recognize our own achievers until they get duly praised and approved by foreigners.

CHAPTER FORTY SIX

When a Track Inspired from the Works of Kalyanji-Anandji Won a Grammy Award

Hindi film music soundtrack bringing home a Grammy has been on the wish list of many renowned Indian artists, though that isn't any kind of requisite to prove their immensely blessed talent, as also widely felt by many veterans. The desperation to have this foreign recognition was mostly seen in the last few decades only and probably that is the reason the original creators of the songs, which eventually won a Grammy after being reused by a foreign Rap Group, didn't even know that the coveted trophy had already been won through a different channel.

To give you the amazing truth, yes, it was an adaptation of two old melodious songs of veteran music director duo Kalyanji-Anandji that did win the Grammy in 2005, through the Rap Group *Black-Eyed-Peas* as a collective effort.

Actually the rap group, after taking the rights through all proper channels, very innovatively used the melody and the actual musical pieces of two Kalyanji-Anandji songs, *Ae Naujawan Hai Sab Kuchh Yahaan* from *Apradh* (1972) and *Yeh Mera Dil Yaar Ka Deewana* from *Don* (1978), both sung by Asha Bhosle, in their track *Don't Phunk With My Heart* released in 2005.

The fresh recreation won them a Grammy in the category of *Best Rap Performance for a Duo or Group* at the 48th Annual Grammy Awards in 2005. Plus, the group duly gave credit for these insertions to their original creators, i.e. the composers Kalyanji-Anandji and the lyricist Indivar, felicitating them in a respectable way celebrating the win in an appreciable spirit.

The winning track begins with an introductory piece taken straight from *Don's* famous track and then follows the basic composition of *Apradh's* song throughout, along with the rap performed by the group as its major component.

So, though not directly, Bollywood music did win a GRAMMY through the *Black Eyed Peas* group's intelligent piece of adaptation or collaboration.

CHAPTER FORTY SEVEN

SHAH RUKH KHAN WAS THERE IN 'MUNNA BHAI M.B.B.S.'

The title is not a mistake, and you have read it perfectly right.

The *Munna Bhai* series is one of the most successful Bollywood series to date, which has been appreciated both by the critics as well as the audience in equal measure. But reportedly the first film of this series, *Munna Bhai MBBS (2003),* was written with Anil Kapoor in mind and then initially planned with the one and only Shah Rukh Khan in the lead that later luckily landed up in the lap of Sanjay Dutt.

As part of the planned project, Shah Rukh was also helpful and contributed with his input while the screenplay of the movie was being written. So though not physically present on the screen, many of the worth-remembering scenes and characterisation are a result of Shah Rukh being there with Rajkumar Hirani and Vidhu Vinod Chopra as a team.

Eventually, due to some reasons beyond their control, Shah Rukh could not become *Munna Bhai* as Sanjay Dutt was destined to play it. But Rajkumar Hirani did not forget to acknowledge the contribution made by Shah Rukh and rightly gave him a humble mention in the film's end credits (mostly missed by the audience while moving out of the theatre).

So next time you watch the film again, just closely look at the credits rolling at the end and you will find:

"Special Thanks to – Shah Rukh Khan: For his inputs in the script"

Indeed, a worth quoting example of sporting spirit to be practiced in any creative medium, including the world of cinema.

❖ ❖ ❖

Fact File: Later in the official biographical film *Sanju* (2018), made on the life of Sanjay Dutt, Hirani prominently included a sequence conveying the fact that it was Sanjay's father, Sunil Dutt, who finally picked up the script of *Munna Bhai MBBS* from the bunch of many and inspired him to go for it first.

CHAPTER FORTY EIGHT

Utpal Dutt's amazing connection with Amitabh Bachchan's career

The veteran thinking artist Utpal Dutt has been part of a few Amitabh Bachchan projects right from the beginning - 1969 to the late '80s. But amazingly there exists a unique connection between the two known figures, which has not been noticed by many.

To begin with, the star of the millennium, Amitabh, had two kinds of debuts in Hindi films. One when he was introduced as a narrator with his famous baritone voice in Mrinal Sen's *Bhuvan Shome* in the year 1969; and two, when he was introduced as a young energetic actor in K. A. Abbas's *Saat Hindustani* (Censored in 1969 and released in 1970), playing one of the seven key characters in its script.

Now the first and the most significant point to be noticed is that in both these prestigious projects, the lead role was played by none other than Utpal Dutt.

Secondly, Dutt played the unusual negative role of the main villain in very few Hindi films, and the three key ventures again happened to be Amitabh Bachchan films. The first was *The Great Gambler* (1979), in which the Bengali veteran played the smuggler/gangster. Second, Barsat Ki Ek Raat (1981) wherein Dutt played a greedy businessman and third, the controversial *Inquilaab* (1984), in which he portrayed the character of a corrupt politician cum businessman. Besides, he also played the subtle negative role of an opportunist film director in Amitabh's *Do Anjaane* (1976).

Continuing the lesser-talked-about relationship, Utpal Dutt probably gave his only screen appearance (cameo) as a Sikh military officer in the Hindi film *Imaan Dharam* (1977), which again had Amitabh playing one of the lead characters along with Shashi Kapoor and Sanjeev Kumar. It is simply an outstanding, worth-watching act in which Dutt suddenly interrupts a politician's speech and performs a spirited song on the stage along with military jawans. The song sequence gives you goosebumps even today when Dutt loses his artificial leg while dancing to the energetic 'Dhol' beats and then goes crawling all the way to pick it up on his own with Sanjeev Kumar sportingly playing the *'dufli'* to inspire him.

Incidentally, just two years later, Amitabh too made a cameo appearance in Dutt's *Golmaal* directed by Hrishikesh Mukherjee in 1979.

However, amazingly this hidden relationship between the two veterans continued post Dutt's sudden demise too when Amitabh featured as the lead actor in Rituparno Ghosh's *The Last Lear* in 2008, which was an English film based on Utpal Dutt's Bengali play *Aajker Shahjahan (Aaj Ke Shahjahan/Today's Shahjahan*) talking about an eccentric Shakespearean actor.

As destiny had planned, the film won the National Award for Best Feature Film in English in 2009, completing an evident circle of *Karma* after four decades since their first film together, *Bhuvan*

Shome, which was also awarded the National Award for the Best Hindi Film in 1969.

In addition, while Dutt won the Best Actor National Award for *Bhuvan Shome,* Amitabh won the Most Promising Newcomer National Award for *Saat Hindustani* in the same year.

Hence, the two undeniably had an extraordinary connection between their careers right from the very beginning.

CHAPTER FORTY NINE

THE VANISHING ACT OF RAKSHA-BANDHAN SONGS FROM OUR HINDI CINEMA

Cinema has always been considered a mirror of society and its people living in different parts of the world and there was a time when scripts of Hindi films were deeply inspired by the roots of Indian traditions and festivals.

Sadly, the fast-changing lifestyle has almost sucked that traditional element out of our Hindi cinema, operating now more or less with an artificial breathing apparatus. The visual, musical, and lyrical representation of our family values and its warm relationships has simply vanished from our film scripts, and we have readily sacrificed all that gold in the blind race of commercialisation moving towards a phony society.

Looking at the films today, the one adorable festival missing from our on-screen portrayals remains *Raksha Bandhan,* which unfortunately does not find its place in any of the major sequences, songs, or even prominent mention in the on-screen proceedings of a storyline.

On the other side, the festival of *Holi* still gets the same attention and is readily included with all its music, colour, and fun element intact (due to the inviting romance involved), which also reveals the hidden mindset of our social structure quite clearly.

Hence, may be not direct but these partial portrayals of emotional festivals have certainly got something to do with the so-called progressive yet questionable new trends we have started following so religiously.

The write-up here simply is to recall that constructive era when there used to be songs, sequences, and even whole films made around this loving brother-sister relationship and the festival of *Raksha Bandhan* celebrating their warm bonding.

In other words, our cinema today has eventually lost the feeling or depth which could say,

"Behna Ne Bhai Ki Kalaai Se Pyaar Baandha Hai,
Resham Ki Dori Se Sansaar Baandha Hai"

(Film: *Resham Ki Dori* (1974), Lyrics: Indivar, Music: Shankar Jaikishan)

And the spirit of expressing the true emotions where the poet could write,

"Shaayad Woh Saawan Bhi Aaye,
Jo Pehla Sa Rang Na Laaye,
Behen Paraye Des Basi Ho,
Agar Woh Tum Tak Pahunch Na Paaye,
Yaad Ka Deepak Jalana…!
Bhaiya Mere Rakhi Ke Bandhan Ko Nibhana,
Bhaiya Mere Chhoti Behen Ko Na Bhulana...
Bhaiya Mere"

(Film: *Chhoti Bahen* (1959), Lyrics: Shailendra, Music: Shankar Jaikishan)

However, life moves on...may be on the surface only, and we continue to live it according to our own choices with the changing times, in the absence of all those values that used to be the backbone of a happy and content life without any new-age hassles or problems.

But still, there is hope...hope which always remains with us unconditionally.

❖ ❖ ❖

Fact File: After a long gap of decades, director Anand L. Rai tried to bring back the emotion on screen with his film *Raksha Bandhan* in 2022 featuring Akshay Kumar in the lead. Sadly, it remained a half-hearted attempt that could not revive the spirit and did not get any appreciation from the audience.

CHAPTER FIFTY

The lost art of Riddle based songs in Hindi film music

Songs based on riddles or brain teasers (*Paheli* in Hindi) used to be quite popular in the golden era of Hindi film music and a few of them are still played in children's programmes in schools even after half a century of their initial release. However, the bitter truth is that the present generation of kids is not familiar with any such song watching the current films, since the trend had vanished long ago before the '90s.

So with the motive of taking you back in time by introducing this particular musical form (which was quite a difficult one, especially for the lyricists), here is a list of all popular 'riddle-based' tracks to give you an instant experience of that golden age of Hindi film music and its master creators.

1. Ichak Daana Beechak Daana Daane Upar Daana

(Shri 420 - 1955) (Lyrics: Hasrat Jaipuri, Music: Shankar Jaikishan, Singers: Lata Mangeshkar and Mukesh)

The song features Nargis teaching the kids as a school teacher and asking them to solve some simple riddles. Raj Kapoor is also enjoying the teaching session from a distance and assumes that he knows all the answers whereas he doesn't. In the end, he asks a riddle too which no one is able to solve, including the teacher, and she gets annoyed. This is probably the most famous song in this particular genre, which many must have heard, enjoyed, and may be performed on as well during their schooldays.

2. Ek Sawaal Main Karun, Ek Sawaal Tum Karo

(Sasural - 1961) (Lyrics: Shailendra, Music: Shankar Jaikishan, Singers: Lata Mangeshkar and Mohd. Rafi)

This song was shot as a stage competition sequence, where Rajendra Kumar and B. Saroja Devi are trying to outshine each other by answering every question with another related question as their reply. Undoubtedly an extremely well-written song by Shailendra based on a unique idea.

3. Bol Gori Bol Tera Kaun Piya

(*Milan* – 1967) *(Lyrics: Anand Bakshi, Music: Laxmikant Pyarelal, Singers: Lata Mangeshkar and Mukesh)*

Conceived as a festival dance song being performed by Sunil Dutt, in front of a temple, the track has devotional lyrics with riddles pointing towards Lord *Shiva*. Therefore, this certainly remains an incomparable triumph by the veteran Anand Bakshi.

4. Saaf Karo Insaaf Karo

(Aashirwad - 1968) (Lyrics: Gulzar, Music: Vasant Desai, Singers: Asha Bhonsle, Hemlata, Ashok Kumar and Harindranath Chattopadhyay)

An energetic folk song with the traditional *Lavni* dance of Maharashtra, this is an over 9-minute-long track where the riddle session is between a group of *Lavni* dancers and the villagers enjoying the show. Here too in the end Ashok Kumar asks a paheli which no one in the dancing group can answer, forcing them to accept their defeat unwillingly. This brilliant culmination of the song certainly makes it a rare precious gem based on folk music.

5. *Woh Kaun Hai Woh Kaun Hai*

(Anjaana - 1969) (Lyrics: Anand Bakshi, Music: Laxmikant Pyarelal, Singers: Lata Mangeshkar and Mukesh)

It's a *Holi* festival song with teams of boys and girls led by Rajendra Kumar and Babita asking each other riddles. The track is shot as a stage show in the film with a colouful picturisation and a catchy composition.

6. *Teetar Ke Do Aage Teetar*

(Mera Naam Joker - 1970) (Lyrics: Hasrat Jaipuri, Music: Shankar Jaikishan, Singers: Asha Bhosle, Mukesh and Simi Grewal)

This is not a completely riddle-based song, with its other part being a game of tongue twisters. Here, the beautiful teacher, Simi Grewal, casually interacts with her adolescent students at a school picnic. A catchy, fun song smartly incorporated in the film's first hour revolving around young kids and their carefree school life.

7. *Mera Raja Beta Boojhe Ek Paheli*

(Anuraag - 1972) (Lyrics: Anand Bakshi, Music: S. D. Burman, Singer: Lata Mangeshkar)

A soft riddle-based song as well as a melodious lullaby, this has a soothing rendition wherein a concerned mother is singing for her son who is suffering from a serious ailment. The song also has a sad version in the film in its tragic climax.

8. Aadhi Roti Saara Kabaab, Bol Mere Murge Kuk-Du-Ku

(Janta Hawaldaar - 1979) (Lyrics: Majrooh Sultanpuri, Music: Rajesh Roshan, Singers: Lata Mangeshkar and Anwar)

This is another fun-filled competition song between a group of girls led by Hema Malini and the innocent Rajesh Khanna playing Janta Hawaldaar, wherein Hema accepts her defeat in the end.

9. Munni Pappu Aur Chunmun

(Arjun - 1985) (Lyrics: Javed, Music: R. D. Burman, Singer: Asha Bhosle)

10. Akkad Bakkad Bombay Bo

(Kirayedar – 1986) (Lyrics: Hasan Kamal, Music: Bappi Lahiri, Singer: Asha Bhosle)

The above two songs are probably the last riddle-based songs in Hindi cinema completing the circle, which started from a similar song of the genre witnessed in *Shri 420.*

In the first song from *Arjun*, we have a gorgeous teacher, Dimple Kapadia, asking riddles to small kids in a kindergarten, and Sunny Deol answers every riddle with only one word – *naukri* (job). The strange, repetitive answers by Sunny superbly denoted the basic theme of the film, which was about the problems faced by the unemployed educated youth in the country.

The second from *Kirayedar* also has a teacher, Padmini Kolhapure singing the riddle song to the kids in a class and Raj Babbar watching her silently.

Interestingly, this was the same situation that was earlier seen in *Shree 420* in the first riddle-based song *Ichak Daana* in 1955. Probably both the directors Rahul Rawail and Basu Chatterji had the hit Raj Kapoor-Nargis song in their mind while conceiving this particular situation in their films released in the mid-1980s.

Apart from the above, there are four more tracks which, though not exactly based on riddles, have an identical format and are worth mentioning here due to their noteworthy musical value.

1. Boojh Mera Kya Naam Re

(CID - 1956) (Lyrics: Majrooh Sultanpuri, Music: O. P. Nayyar, Singer: Shamshad Begum)

This has a village girl singing the song along with her group as they are on their way to fetch water.

2. Woh Kya Hai, Ik Mandir Hai

(Anuraag - 1972) (Lyrics: Anand Bakshi, Music: S. D. Burman, Singer: Lata Mangeshkar and Mohd. Rafi)

A touching creation, wherein a blind girl is asking questions from her beloved (with a normal vision) about various things around that she can feel through her other instincts. This is one of the most meaningful and soothing songs in this rare genre, originally based on a Bengali track.

3. Chand Kya Hai, Roop Ka Darpan

(Dhamkee – 1973) (Lyrics: Asad Bhopali, Music: Ganesh, Singer: Asha Bhosle and Kishore Kumar)

It is a love song picturised on Vinod Khanna and Kumkum, in which they ask simple questions about various things to each other. The film also had a special appearance by Subhash Ghai (as an actor).

4. Naino Mein Darpan Hai Darpan Mein Koi

(Aarop – 1974) (Lyrics: Maya Govind, Music: Bhupen Hazarika, Singer: Lata Mangeshkar and Kishore Kumar)

It's a melodious track featuring Vinod Khanna and Saira Banu questioning each other about the meaning of the words Sajan and Sajini.

Concluding the write-up, it is really unfortunate that we have lost this art of making melodious, enjoyable songs based on interesting riddles, maybe because the pace of life has now become so fast, making us all incapable of cherishing such innocent expressions.

CHAPTER FIFTY ONE

BOLD HINDI FILMS DEALING WITH THE CONTROVERSIAL AND SHOCKING THEME OF INCEST

Since the beginning of the last century, Hindi cinema has mostly been about routine and comfortable subjects with quite rare exceptions to the rule, and that too witnessed more towards the last few decades post the '90s. But surprisingly one of the most controversial and shocking subjects of *Incest* (consensual or non-consensual physical relationship between close relatives, largely considered a crime/not to be confused with child abuse) was adapted in an indicative way even in the pre-independence era during the early '40s and since then has been a part of many mainstream projects as mentioned below.

1. ***Bharosa* (1940):** Probably the first Hindi film based on this unexpectedly bold theme, *Bharosa* – directed by Sohrab Modi – revolved around two friendly men, a woman, and their kids, who later marry each other unaware of the reality of being brother and sister. A film

dealing with betrayal, guilt, and suicide was praised by the reputed magazine Filmindia in its review despite calling it flawed with mediocre execution.

2. ***Bahen* (1941):** Directed by one of the most respected film-makers of Indian Cinema, Mehboob Khan, the film is about an obsessive brother who does not wish his sister to leave him even after her marriage. Though in my opinion, the film does not deal with the subject directly, still it is considered as indicating the same by many. However, it is quite possible that the reference to incest might have surfaced in the later decades with the so-called development of our questionable social structure and over-analytical mindsets.
3. ***Bambai Ka Babu* (1960):** Written by Rajinder Singh Bedi, this had a script similar to O. Henry's short story *A Double-Dyed Deceiver,* which had an imposter living with a family posing to be their son. But as an added plot, the musical masterpiece had Dev Anand romancing the gorgeous Suchitra Sen who is supposed to be his sister, being the daughter of the same family.
4. ***Prem Shastra* (1974):** Dealing with the theme of incest in a bold and in-your-face manner, *Prem Shastra* once again had Dev Anand having a physical relationship with Zeenat Aman, who later turns out to be the daughter of his cunning wife but from a different man, who is none other than his elder brother.
5. ***Mausam* (1975)**: The film had only a subtle indication of the subject when Sanjeev Kumar finds his young daughter Sharmila Tagore working at a brothel, having a stark resemblance to her dead mother. Meeting her, he is in dilemma about how to deal with this disturbing

fact and bring her back to his house, saving her from that ugly hell.

6. ***Zameer* (1975):** Having a storyline almost identical to the above-mentioned *Bambai Ka Babu* (1960), *Zameer* had Amitabh Bachchan playing the imposter son in a rich businessman's (Shammi Kapoor) house. But there he is introduced to Saira Banu as his sister, with whom he was having a romantic relationship in the film's first hour.
7. ***Mandi* (1983)** – Based on a classic Urdu short story *Anandi* by Ghulam Abbas, *Mandi* talks about the collective life lived by several women in a brothel running in the center of a small city. The young boy of a local politician falls in love with a beautiful virgin girl (Smita Patil) at that brothel, who in reality is his sister as the father of that girl happens to be the politician himself.
8. ***Ek Nai Paheli* (1984)**: Talking about love between two individuals of different age groups, this is a complex tale of a few unusual relationships that develop when the hero (Kamal Hassan) leaves his home (after an argument with his father) to live with a beautiful middle-aged lady (a singer). In an interesting turn of events, the young rebellious daughter of that singer lady starts having a live-in affair with the hero's father, heading towards a marriage. No doubt it is complex enough to understand in just a few lines.
9. ***Triyacharitra* (1994)** – In this offbeat venture based on Shiv Murti's novel with the same title, a poor and innocent girl is not only raped by her cunning father-in-law but also blamed for the shameful act by the ignorant village *Panchayat*, highlighting the sad state of Indian women in rural areas.

10. ***Fire* (1996):** Deepa Mehta's famous movie, which was widely opposed in India at the time of its release, had neglected wives of two brothers living in the same house breaking the traditional norms of the society and developing a lesbian relationship without feeling any kind of regret whatsoever.
11. ***Hum Deewane Pyar Ke* (2001):** A confused mother refuses to approve the girl her young son wants to marry as she doubts that the father of that girl might be her husband, whom she assumed to be dead many years ago during a political upheaval.
12. ***Everybody Says I'm Fine* (2001):** A young man running a unisex parlour accidentally gets the power to read his clients' weird thoughts. During one of his sessions, he comes to know about a beautiful girl having an incestual relationship with her sick father.
13. ***Matrubhoomi* (2003):** One of the most hard-hitting realistic films from Indian cinema focusing on the alarmingly serious problem of girl foeticide, this award-winning gem sarcastically portrayed the issue in a blunt manner. It talked about a family of all men (five brothers and their father) who mutually decide to share the wife of their elder brother, taking turns to sleep with her on the day of the week assigned to them, shockingly also including the father-in-law. It is a film that can easily make the sick Indian mindset feel disgustingly shameful like never before.
14. ***Janani* (2006)** – A young boy is denied the approval to marry a middle-class girl because, in reality, she is his sister. Actually, the girl's mother had served as the surrogate mother for the young boy's family and it was the same boy who was born to her in the past.

15. ***Undertrial* (2007)** – Reportedly based on a true incident, it revolves around a poor man who is accused of raping his three young daughters, with the charges filed by his wife. A debut attempt by the director, the film did manage to raise many eyebrows but couldn't reach the majority of the audience due to its dark & sadistic theme.
16. ***Thanks Maa* (2010)** – A worth-watching, thoughtful film about an infant child left alone by his mother and later taken care of by a group of street kids. However, when the leader of the gang of street boys somehow finds the real mother, then he comes to know that the girl had left the child to die as it was the result of the helpless physical relationship with her father.
17. ***The Girl In The Yellow Boots* (2010)** – A bold film revealing the shocking truth found by a girl, desperately searching for her father. The father, who was a sex maniac abusing his daughters in their early childhood, is now looking for some kind of spiritual solace in various cities, ashrams, and even a massage parlour. He accidentally visits the one where his daughter is working as the masseuse.

Apart from the above, some brutal rapes by close relatives and references of incestuous relationships also featured in *Bhanwar* (1947), *Phagun* (1973), *Ishq Ishq Ishq* (1974), *Kalyug* (1981), *Ek Chadar Maili Si* (1986), *Hamara Khandaan* (1988), *Yateem* (1988), *Na-mumkin* (1988), *Waaris* (1988), *Clerk* (1989), *Devki* (2006), *Silsilay* (2005), *Water* (2005) and *My Birthday Song* (2018). Moreover, the theme was in the news for a film titled *I Am Roshni* (2017-18), which revolved around the relationship between a brother and sister, and most recently, it was also there in *Yes Papa,* released in 2024.

Expectedly, none of the mentioned films could witness any degree of huge success at the box office due to their unpleasant and dark themes showcasing the brutal truth, which is often pushed under the carpet out of shame, disgust, and regret. Perhaps that is why a handful of films from the above list tried to justify their weird storyline by adding some sane adjustments, making them more acceptable to Indian audiences.

Still, these remain daring attempts by their respective filmmakers, who went ahead with such experimental projects that were bound to meet an adverse fate at the box office for obvious reasons.

A Note of Thanks

This book would not have been possible without the constant encouragement showered by the supportive readers on my website and everyone on the social networks namely Facebook, Twitter, and Instagram. Your kind and appreciative comments gave me the courage and spirit to compile the selected posts on my website and new articles in the form of a book to reach more fellow lovers of Hindi cinema all over the globe.

Collection of many old classic movies, music albums, special editions of vintage film magazines, reputed website portals, and valuable information provided by a few learned friends remain the major source of the content shared in these 51 chapters. So, I am hugely indebted and thankful to everyone who spent their hard-earned money and precious time to go through my sincere effort.

Hope I was able to provide what you were searching for and God willing this turns out to be a stepping stone and with your appreciation leads to many more volumes in the series in the coming future.

With warm wishes for everyone and their loved ones too.

Cheers!

HIS BLESSINGS

Author Bio – Bobby Sing

Beginning the journey, exploring avenues as a stage artist, musician, poet, educationist, and graphic designer, the author is now an experienced critic, creative-music consultant, and a prolific writer on cinema – active in the field since the late 90s.

With the real name of *Harpreet Singh*, his everlasting relationship with cinema began with the nickname *Bobby,* inspired by Raj Kapoor's cult film released in the early '70s. His passion for cinema flourished while working with music and home video companies when the Audio-VCD-DVD market was at its peak in India. As a columnist on cinema, he has been associated with reputed publications such as Indo-US Dialogue Magazine, Network 18, Free Press Journal, and more along with being active as a creative-script-music consultant in Hindi and Punjabi Cinema.

As an author, his 'Did You Know' series of books is specifically conceived for all the young friends, who are more than eager to know about the present as well as the past classics of our Hindi cinema and the lesser-known stories related to their making. Vol.1 of this series is also available in Hindi with the title *"Itna To Yaad Hai Mujhe"* published by Prabhat Prakashan.

Presently Bobby Sing is into creative consultancy, music production, and writing columns/reviews/articles on Indian Cinema for reputed publications apart from being active on his personal website.

He has recently contributed as an author to reputed books such as *GUIDE, The Film: Perspectives,* published by Blue Pencil, and *The Swinging Seventies: Stars, Style and Substance in Hindi Cinema,* published by Om Books International.

Website: www.bobbytalkscinema.com

E-Mail: bobbysing@gmail.com

www.facebook.com/imbobbysing

www.twitter.com/bobbytalkcinema

www.instagram/bobbytalkscinema

25 Recommended Reads on the Subject

1. Satyajit Ray The Inner Eye – Andrew Robinson
2. Our Films Their Films – Satyajit Ray
3. The Complete Adventures of Feluda (1 & 2) – Satyajit Ray
4. Travails With The Alien – Satyajit Ray – Edited by Sandip Ray
5. Mansarover – Premchand's Famous Stories – Premchand
6. Romancing with Life – Dev Anand
7. The Navketan Story : Cinema Modern – Sidharth Bhatia
8. Guide – R. K. Narayan
9. Chetan Anand: The Poetics of Film – Uma Anand – Ketan Anand
10. Bobby The Complete Story – K. A. Abbas
11. Mera Naam Joker The Complete Story – K. A. Abbas
12. The Making of Don – Krishna Gopalan
13. Pakeezah – Meghnad Desai
14. Libaas – Gulzar
15. Leave Disco Dancer Alone – Sudha Rajagopalan
16. Disco Dancer : A Comedy In Five Acts – Anuvab Pal
17. Conversations with Gulzar – Nasreen Munni Kabir
18. Echoes & Eloquences :The Life and Cinema of Gulzar – Saibal Chatterjee
19. Utpal Dutt on Cinema – Utpal Dutt

20. Enchantment of The Mind : Manmohan Desai's Films – Connie Haham
21. Gaata Rahe Mera Dil – Anirudha Bhattacharjee & Balaji Vittal
22. Conversations with Waheeda Rehman – Nasreen Munni Kabir
23. Raj Kapoor: The Fabulous Showman – Bunny Reuben
24. Amar Akbar Anthony : Masala, Madness, Manmohan Desai – Sidharth Bhatia
25. S.D.Burman: The Prince-Musician – Anirudha Bhattacharjee & Balaji Vittal